TABLE OF CONTENTS

Top 20 Test Taking Tips

1. Carefully follow all the test registration procedures
2. Know the test directions, duration, topics, question types, how many questions
3. Setup a flexible study schedule at least 3-4 weeks before test day
4. Study during the time of day you are most alert, relaxed, and stress free
5. Maximize your learning style; visual learner use visual study aids, auditory learner use auditory study aids
6. Focus on your weakest knowledge base
7. Find a study partner to review with and help clarify questions
8. Practice, practice, practice
9. Get a good night's sleep; don't try to cram the night before the test
10. Eat a well balanced meal
11. Know the exact physical location of the testing site; drive the route to the site prior to test day
12. Bring a set of ear plugs; the testing center could be noisy
13. Wear comfortable, loose fitting, layered clothing to the testing center; prepare for it to be either cold or hot during the test
14. Bring at least 2 current forms of ID to the testing center
15. Arrive to the test early; be prepared to wait and be patient
16. Eliminate the obviously wrong answer choices, then guess the first remaining choice
17. Pace yourself; don't rush, but keep working and move on if you get stuck
18. Maintain a positive attitude even if the test is going poorly
19. Keep your first answer unless you are positive it is wrong
20. Check your work, don't make a careless mistake

Foundations of Reading Development

Children's literacy development

Infants begin literacy development when they hear language spoken to and around them. They become aware of speech as a medium of communication. Soon, they are also exposed to children's books and begin to develop print awareness, including discriminating between speech and print. This first stage of literacy development is known as the stage of awareness and exploration. Parents can support this stage by reading aloud to babies from board books with bright colors and large, simple images. Reading them poems, including nursery rhymes, also helps as their repetition attracts infants' attention. Babies learn by exploring their environment; toddlers, with their increased locomotion, expand their exploration. Parents can help them learn language by associating environmental objects with their word names. Pointing to things and asking "What's that?" is an effective game for learning vocabulary. In this stage, children also develop letter recognition and association of letters with the phonemes (speech sounds) that they represent.

From the first stage of literacy development in which babies and toddlers develop awareness and exploration of spoken and printed language, they become preschool children and move into the stage of experimental reading and writing. During this time, children are typically learning to sing the "Alphabet Song," whereby they memorize every letter in the alphabet. They are learning to associate certain letters and the sounds that they represent with words most significant in their lives, such as the spelling of their names and their parents' names, and the numbers and words in their home addresses. At this age, preschool children are typically very interested in looking at books. Parents can take advantage of this natural motivation by continuing to read aloud to their children every day, and also encouraging them to read words out of the books themselves. At this stage, children are also likely to start scribbling, producing written letters and numbers, and write their own names. Parents can provide challenges by pointing at signs outdoors and having children name their letters.

Babies and toddlers first develop awareness and exploration of spoken and printed language; preschoolers develop experimental reading and writing skills. Once they begin kindergarten and first grade, children are in the early learning reading and writing stage; these skills are further developed by formal schooling. In school, children typically learn phonics, i.e., recognizing the speech sounds (phonemes) associated with letters and being able to combine two or more phonemes and letters to create words. Because their orientation is primarily phonetic or sound-oriented rather than orthographic or spelling-oriented at this point, it is common and normal for children to spell phonetically rather than according to orthographic conventions. For example, many children will write "pikcher" to represent the sounds of the word spelled "picture." Additional developments during this stage include children now understanding that printed words are separated from other words by spaces; and that they understand the concept of sentences constructed from words.

The first stage of literacy development is awareness and exploration of spoken and written language; the second involves experimenting with reading and writing; and the third focuses on the early learning of reading and writing in the formal education setting. The fourth stage is considered one of transitional reading and writing, typically during the second and third grades of elementary school. Children can not only associate printed words and sentences with spoken language; moreover, they can now also recognize the meanings of printed words and can read on their own. In this stage, they are starting to gain an understanding of the significance of written language, and their reading comprehension improves. At this time, children typically can read a statement and comprehend its main thesis. They can combine multiple ideas to understand the overall "big picture." Parents and teachers can help children better comprehend the books they read independently, by suggesting that they relate the stories to their own lives.

Babies and toddlers (stage 1) develop awareness of spoken and written language and explore its uses in their environments. Preschoolers (stage 2) experiment with early reading and writing, and children entering formal school settings (stage 3) learn further literacy skills. By the fourth stage of transitional literacy, second and third graders gain greater reading comprehension and begin to read independently. The fifth stage is considered that of competent reading and writing, which typically develops by fourth grade and thereafter. By this time, children are skilled enough at reading that they can learn and comprehend new or unfamiliar words, including those that are complex. They are able to read long novels rather than just short stories. They can comprehend the meanings and themes in the reading without adult help. As children become older, they may develop more or less interest in reading; however, their reading skills are maintained from this stage onward. Adults can encourage children's continued motivation to read by providing them with books on subjects that individually interest them.

Speech and writing

When we study speech, we are studying the sounds we produce and hear for communication. When we study writing, we are studying the visual symbols we produce and see for communication. Yet in language, these two separate modalities are related: people (except in Deaf culture) learn to read and write through relating visual symbols to speech sounds. For correct spelling, the two modalities of speech and writing must come together. However, it is inaccurate to regard writing, as many people do, as simply speech put in writing: rules are stricter for writing than for speech, and speech incorporates vocal cues to meaning that writing cannot. However, many people also judge speech according to writing, which is also inaccurate. For example, many written words contain "silent" letters not voiced, and many words are spelled differently from how they sound. Moreover, despite the importance of speech for social interactions, our society places value on the standards set by our written language, as well as its global provenance and more lasting nature.

Phonemic awareness

Phonemic awareness consists of being able to hear, identify, and manipulate individual speech sounds or phonemes. The manipulation of speech sounds includes such processes as breaking words down to individual components; blending phonemes and words; and stretching them. For children to read printed language, they must first develop phonemic awareness. This enables their understanding that words are composed of phonemes, which are the smallest units of sound in a spoken word that affect its meaning. For example, changing the phoneme /s/ to /m/ changes the word sat to mat, a different word and meaning. Children can demonstrate phonemic awareness by identifying words in a group that start with the same phoneme, such as book, boy, and bicycle. They can isolate and pronounce the initial or final phoneme in a word, such as /d/ or /g/ in dog. They can blend phonemes to say a word, e.g. "/d/, /o/, /g/--dog." They can conversely segment words into phonemes, e.g. "dog--/d/, /o/, /g/."

Alphabetic principle

The alphabetic principle is the concept that letters represent speech sounds, and arrangements of letters represent spoken words. When children learn the predictable, systematic relationships of letters to sounds, they can apply their knowledge of these relationships both to words they know and to new words. This enables them to develop reading fluency. Children's treating words as series of letters and remembering written word forms correlate highly with their knowing the shapes and names of letters. Children seem to acquire alphabetic knowledge in this sequence: first, they learn letter names, by singing the alphabet song and reciting alphabetic rhymes; then, they learn letter shapes, by playing with 3-dimensional wood or plastic letters, lettered blocks, and alphabetic books; and then, they learn letter sounds as they relate the letters they see to the speech sounds that they hear and produce. Instruction in phonics assists children in learning and applying the alphabetic principle by explicitly relating visible written letters to audible spoken sounds.

Teaching the alphabetic principle

To help young children understand the relationship between speech sounds and written letters, i.e., the alphabetic principle, teachers should instruct them in letter-sound correspondences in isolation, one pair at a time, and teach these directly and explicitly. Teachers should also integrate in their daily lessons, in all subjects, plenty of opportunities for children to practice the letter-sound relationships they have been explicitly teaching in isolation. Teachers should both review cumulatively all the letter-sound correspondences they have already taught with children, and introduce new sound-letter relationships into both their isolated, direct, explicit lessons and into the opportunities they provide them with for practicing. Early in their instruction and frequently, teachers should give young children ample opportunities for applications of their growing repertoires of sound-letter correspondences by providing them with words whose meanings are familiar to the children, and spelling these phonetically.

According to research, more teacher-directed, explicit instructional methods are more effective than indirect and implicit techniques. Many teachers combine various instructional methods. Teachers should keep in mind that individual children vary in the rates at which they learn sound-to-letter correspondences. Educators find a reasonable rate for introducing new sound-to-letter relationships to be between two and four pairs per week. Consonants and vowels should be introduced in an order that allows children to read words as quickly as possible. The earliest relationships teachers that should introduce are those between the letters and sounds that are used the most in the language. When introducing consonant letters and sounds, teachers should separate single consonant sounds from consonant clusters and blends by putting these in different lessons. They should not introduce letters that look similar and/or sounds that sound similar at the same time. And they should give instruction in blending using words containing letter-sound correspondences that the children have already learned.

Instruction in phonics and the alphabetic principle

Teachers should base their instructional rates on the group performance of their class. While there is no set rule about order of introduction, educators agree that letter-sound relationships with the highest utility—meaning they help children start reading words as soon as possible—should be taught first. For example, the letters a, s, m, t, and p have high utility in our language, while gh in through, x in box, a in want, and ey in they have lower utility and can be taught later. Consonants that are continuous, such as /s/, /f/, /m/, /n/, and /r/, are easier for children to produce in isolation than stops such as /b/, /p/, /g/, /k/, /d/, /t/; and continuous consonants that are initial or medial in words are easier for children to blend than stops in these positions. Visually confusing letters such as /b/ and /p/ or /p/ and /g/, and auditorily confusing sounds such as /b/ and /v/ or /i/ and /e/, should be taught separately. Instruction should match children's learning rates.

Phonological processing

Listening and speech vs. reading and spelling
When we are listening to speech and/or speaking, our phonological processing is largely unconscious. The primary task of listening is to comprehend the meaning of speech, and that of speaking is to convey comprehensible meaning, for communicative purposes rather than to focus on the speech sounds produced; so phonological processing is automatic. In contrast, reading and spelling written language involve more metalinguistic processes (i.e., thinking about and understanding how we use language); these do not come naturally and are not learned easily. However, phonological skills are not highly correlated with intelligence. Some individuals with high cognitive abilities have deficits in phonological awareness. The correlation between phonological awareness and learning to read and write, though, is much stronger in any alphabetically-based written language, and also in non-alphabetic written languages, such as Chinese and Japanese, which are ideographic.

Phonemic awareness informs student understanding of alphabet letters as representing speech sounds

Children cannot decipher our writing/printing system, its patterns, or its representation of spoken language without phonemic awareness. For example, if you ask a child who has not developed good phonemic awareness to tell you the first sound in the word dog, they may say "Bow-wow!" Until they can identify the phoneme /d/ in dog, good, and Dad, and isolate it from these words' other sounds, children cannot understand what the letter d stands for in the words. Research consistently finds that we can predict quite accurately whether children will later read well or poorly, even before they learn to read, by testing their awareness of phonemes in words, their knowledge of letter names, their knowledge of sound-to-letter correspondences, and their vocabulary. Research also finds that the majority—at least 80%—of poor readers also show weak phonological awareness and/or phonological memory; and poor spelling is associated with phonological processing deficits. Studies also find that direct, explicit instruction in phonemic awareness remediates reading and spelling problems and speeds alphabetic learning.

Ways in which phonological awareness and memory both enhance and interact with children's word consciousness and vocabulary development

When students pay attention to words that they do not know, their phonological awareness and their memories are activated as they compare the unfamiliar/new words to words that they already know, which helps them to comprehend and pronounce the new ones. When they hear a new word, their ability to repeat it and pronounce it correctly also depends upon their phonological awareness and their memories. When students hear or read new words, they must be able to encode them correctly in order to remember them; in turn, they must be able to remember them to retrieve them and use them appropriately in their speech and writing. In addition, when students hear words that are similar in sound, they must be able to differentiate between or among them in order to determine their respective meanings. Without good phonological awareness and memory, students are more apt to confuse words that have completely different meanings if they are similar in sound.

Components of knowledge in preschoolers whose presence or absence strongly predicts how easily they will learn to read

Children are predicted to learn to read well in first grade when, as preschoolers, they have developed: (1) recognition of the letters of the alphabet, and the ability to name them; (2) general print knowledge, such as recognizing the front and the back of a book and knowing how to turn its pages; and (3) phonemic awareness, i.e., recognizing, differentiating and manipulating the individual speech sounds/phonemes in words. Giving younger children exposure, experience, information, guidance, and practice with reading builds these three skills. Therefore, parents should read aloud to their babies from birth onward, and read aloud together with them as they develop the abilities to repeat what parents read, to identify letters in words, and to associate some letters with certain speech sounds. Reading aloud with children is the most important activity parents can do to prepare their preschoolers to read. Indeed, many children begin learning to read through this activity before they enter school.

Aspects of social interaction that influence how children learn to read

The ways that parents communicate with their young children influence how the children learn to listen and speak, which contains many of the skills necessary to reading and is strongly correlated with their learning to read. For example, when parents and caregivers sing rhyming songs and play word games with young children, they are developing the children's phonemic awareness. When a very young child just learning to speak has heard and recognizes the word "cookie" and knows what it means and when s/he attempts to produce it and says "cook," her parent responds, "Do you want a cookie?" This helps the child construct knowledge of meaning; reasons for communicating; vocabulary; syntax; and sentence structure. This knowledge will support the child's later reading skills. Early identification of and intervention for hearing, speech, and/or language deficits in young children are crucial for preventing future reading problems.

Reading fluency and non-fluent reading

Reading fluency is an ability to read printed text with speed, accuracy, and (when reading aloud) appropriate expression. Fluent readers automatically recognize the words in a text when they read it silently. To derive meaning from what they are reading, they use strategies such as quickly grouping words into phrases, clauses, and sentences. When fluent readers read text out loud, they do so without effort, and they use natural-sounding vocal expression the same way as when they are speaking spontaneously. Non-fluent readers, in contrast, read slowly and laboriously, one word at a time. When reading aloud, they sound choppy rather than smooth. Fluent readers decode words effortlessly and automatically, identifying and understanding words simultaneously—freeing their attention to focus on the meaning. They form connections among the concepts presented in the text, and between these and their prior knowledge. Readers less fluent divert too much attention to decoding words, so they have little left to focus on understanding the meaning.

Development of reading fluency

Students develop reading fluency gradually, through much practice and time. The oral reading of students whose reading development is in the earliest stage is slow and effortful because they are first learning how to associate letters with sounds and to blend the letter sounds into identifiable words. When students achieve the ability to identify many words automatically, their reading aloud is still not fluent if they read without expression. In order to incorporate expression, readers need the ability to divide the text into "chunks" of meaningful information. They also need to know when to pause during and between sentences, which words to emphasize, and when to change vocal tones. For example, as the Partnership for Reading points out, a fluent reader will read this line from Brown Bear, Brown Bear by Bill Martin Jr. with appropriate pauses and intonation: "Brown bear/Brown bear/What do you see?" while a non-fluent reader will read it, likely in a monotone voice, with misplaced pauses: "Brown/bear brown/bear what/do/you see."

Levels of reading fluency

The three levels of reading fluency are the Frustration, Instructional, and Independent levels. At the Frustration level, the text is hard for the student to read and s/he will attain lower than 90% accuracy in decoding words. At the Instructional level, the text is challenging for the reader but not frustrating, and the reader achieves 90% word accuracy. At the Independent level, the student finds the text relatively easy to read and attains 95% accuracy in recognizing and understanding its words. Fluency instruction should utilize text that the student can read at his/her Independent reading level. This is because students can focus on practicing reading speed and expression, instead of on decoding words, at their Independent levels. Fluency is not a fixed stage where readers can read all words easily and rapidly; it varies with text and subject familiarity. For example, even students who normally read very fluently may read slowly and laboriously with highly technical text on an unfamiliar subject, such as medical journal articles or nuclear physics textbooks.

Repeated and monitored oral reading

In repeated and monitored oral reading, students read and re-read text passages aloud several times, with their teacher providing feedback and guidance to correct and enhance fluency in their subsequent re-readings. This considerably improves their word recognition, reading speed, and reading accuracy along with their reading fluency. It additionally improves reading comprehension. Repeated reading is effective in elementary grades and remedially helpful for upper-grade students struggling with reading. Teachers have often traditionally used "round-robin" reading, wherein students take turns reading parts of a text, for developing oral reading fluency. However, this is not effective for fluency, because students read too small a portion of text, and because they do not read it repeatedly. Research finds that reading and re-reading orally until they reach an acceptable fluency level—typically four times for most students—is more effective. Judiciously designed feedback on reader performance during repeated readings gives the reader guidance. Using tutors, peers, audio recordings, etc., can also augment practice with reading aloud.

Silent, independent reading

Much research has revealed a strong correlation between a student's reading ability and the amount of time that the student spends reading. In fact, how much time they spend reading is considered one of the primary differences between poor and good readers. Because of these conclusions, experts have advised teachers for many years to encourage students to read voluntarily in classrooms. The literature in reading education and teacher education frequently offers classroom procedures, such as Silent Sustained Reading (SSR) and Drop Everything and Read (DEAR), to motivate students to read independently. However, research does not show that reading silently and independently with little or no feedback or guidance yields any improvement in reading fluency or achievement. Instead, studies find direct reading instruction to be most predictive of reading achievement. Nevertheless, teachers should not overlook the importance of providing students with time to read silently from books they can read at their Independent fluency level—i.e., they can read them with 95% word accuracy—to apply their reading skills.

Orthography

Orthography means spelling. Traditional spelling instruction concentrated on memorizing; however, research findings about orthographic layers inform moving away from memorizing to the word study approach. In word study, students learn through "word work," various hands-on activities teachers assign for exploring three layers of orthography: alphabetic, pattern, and meaning. In studying the alphabetic layer, students match letters and letter pairs (such as sh, th, ch) with corresponding sounds and form words from them. When studying the pattern layer, they find larger patterns in letter groupings—for example, the consonant-vowel-consonant-final e (CVCe) pattern in words such as love, hate, more, move, fine, face, etc. When they study the semantic layer, students come to understand how spelling reflects semantic relationships; for instance, composition is spelled with a medial o because it is derived from compose. Studying orthographic layers helps students understand how written words operate by enabling them to identify their derivations, patterns, and regularities; and helps them strategically apply this information for decoding new words and writing with correct spelling.

Morphology

Morphology is the study of word structure as formed from the smallest units of meaning, called morphemes. A morpheme can be as small as the letter s, when added to a singular noun to make it plural, such as cat + s = cats. Changing morphemes can change the meaning of both a word and its sentence. For instance, "Mother bake**s** cookies" means she does this in the present tense, and/or in general. Changing -s to -ed yields "Mother bak**ed** cookies," meaning she did this in the past. Letter groups like roots, prefixes and suffixes are also morphemes. For example, the words progress, egress, and digress all contain the same "gress" root from Latin gradi, to go, with different prefixes: pro meaning forward, i.e., go forward; e meaning out, i.e. go out or exit; and di (from dis) meaning away or aside from, i.e.

to go away from the subject. Students understanding morphemes can more easily discern word meanings, and decode complex new words through recognizing their morphological parts

Semantics

Semantics refers to word meanings. Knowing more word definitions and knowing some single words have multiple meanings enhances reading comprehension and fluency. Semantic feature analysis helps students to grasp important concepts and make connections and predictions. It also improves their skills in reading comprehension and vocabulary development. This strategy shows both similarities and differences in words and emphasizes each word's uniqueness. Moreover, it activates students' previous knowledge, and it reveals information about word meanings through discussion. It is used before, during, and after reading with individual students, small groups, and whole classes. The teacher chooses a topic/category; gives the students key topic aspects and vocabulary words; and makes a chart with topic features across the top and vocabulary words down the left side. Students mark a + sign for vocabulary words fitting a topic feature and a − sign for those not fitting it; or a blank if unknown. For example, in language arts, students might compare book genres; in science, students might compare/contrast characteristics of different kinds of dinosaurs.

Influence of written language on children's motivation to learn to read

One factor that is required for children's motivation to learn to read is their understanding and appreciation of the functions and purposes of written language. They must develop awareness of the presence of printed language surrounding them in the environment—not just in books, magazines, and newspapers, but also on labels, billboards, traffic signs, street signs, directional signs, store signs, etc. Accompanying this awareness, children must realize that these various forms of print serve a great many different purposes. In reading and writing, some instructional activities that support children's understanding and appreciation of written language include: activities helping children realize that print represents spoken language; activities highlighting the uses, production, and meanings of print in classroom directions, notes, posters, calendars, labels, and signs; and activities teaching directionality and other print conventions. Other instructional activities that support children's understanding and appreciation of written language include: activities giving children practice in handling books (finding front and back covers, page tops and bottoms, turning pages); activities using patterned, predictable stories to give children practice; and word awareness lessons building knowledge of word appearances, lengths, and boundaries

Role of context in influencing purpose and constructing meaning in reading and writing

The physical, social, and cultural contexts in which writers and readers operate shapes the decisions made by writers in composing their texts; and the decisions made by readers in constructing meaning from those texts as they read them. The context surrounding a writer influences, and even determines, that writer's purposes for writing what s/he does and how s/he writes it. Additionally, the choices made by writers are influenced by the limitations, opportunities, and requirements available, which themselves are influenced by the writers' contexts. Context affects readers' efforts to construct meaning from writers' work as they read it. The reader's physical context can make their ability to read a text better or worse. A reader's social context influences how many experiences and expectations, and which ones, the reader shares in common with the writer of the text s/he is reading. And cultural context influences the basic beliefs, assumptions, and desires that a writer incorporates into a text; and those that a reader brings when reading it, affecting his/her interpretation.

Learning the foundations for reading and writing

Children begin learning and experimenting with language in their earliest months. Infants' babbling emulates the vocal tones, rhythms, and expression of adult speech. Very young children start making associations between words they hear and what they represent. When they enjoy playing "peek-a-boo," "patty-cake," and similar interactive games; listening to familiar rhymes and songs; and manipulating letter blocks and board books, they are learning to employ various symbols. At the same time, they learn that print also symbolizes meanings. As they begin to understand the alphabetic principle, they cognitively process the letters they encounter, convert them to sounds, and associate the letters and sounds with meaning. While, to some observers, it can appear that some children seem to gain such understanding "magically" or independently, research is more suggestive that adults have given them much instruction and guidance, even if they do so informally and playfully. Children's early years are also characterized by diverse experiences with spoken and written language.

Linguistic experiences encountered by young children

Researchers have identified significantly diverse, linguistic experiences encountered by young children, at home, during child care, and in social situations. Studies have found that children meet with many different kinds of linguistic resources and different degrees and kinds of support for their early experiences and learning of reading and writing. While some children are provided with easy access to ample ranges of reading and writing materials, other children have less access. Some children often observe their parents reading and writing, while other children rarely or never see this. Some children are given informal, casual support, while others are given direct instruction by adults. The implication of this variety is that there is no single teaching approach or method that can be expected to be most efficacious for every child. Competent teachers instead utilize many different teaching strategies to address the diversity among children found in schools. Instruction should build on children's existing knowledge and abilities. It should also furnish children with skills, knowledge, and attitudes, and habits promoting life-long learning.

General areas about which young children need to learn regarding reading and writing

Children need to learn about the technical skills involved in reading and writing. Moreover, they need to learn how to employ these skills as tools to improve their thinking and reasoning skills. Numerous studies identify reading aloud to children as the one most important activity for developing skills and understanding required for successful reading and writing. Research has found that when children feel emotionally secure and also participate actively in reading, the result is a high quality of book reading. Teachers or caregivers working with small groups are found to enhance children's comprehension and vocabulary by asking questions requiring analysis and prediction. Children can discuss pictures in books, retell the stories read, identify their favorite parts, and often ask for repeated re-readings (a typical characteristic of young children). Discussion empowers children to connect stories with their own lives. One researcher (Snow, 1991) described such discussions as, "decontextualized language," wherein teachers can stimulate higher-order cognition by helping children bridge story events from what they see, to what they can imagine.

Objective to pursue with preschool-aged children to support their learning to read and write

At preschool ages, much research supports that optimizing children's exposure to printed language and their ideas about it is an essential objective. One way teachers do this is to use Big Books to assist young children in noticing and differentiating many features of print. For example, they can help children realize that it is not the pictures, but the print, that delivers the story's meaning. They can show them how series of letters are words; that printed words represent spoken words; and that we read printed English from left to right and top to bottom. While reading stories with young children, teachers can point out specific words; guide children's attention to where the reading begins; and give children assistance in recognizing the shapes and sounds of different letters. Indeed, these ways in which teachers demonstrate how print functions have been identified by some researchers as being the keys to developing word awareness and other concepts that are crucial to children for learning to read and write.

Physically arranging classrooms to support using books

In addition to teachers' instructional strategies and the activities they design for children to participate in with print, children additionally must be given opportunities to practice what they have learned, by themselves and with their peers. Research finds that physical classroom arrangement can support children's spending more time using books. For example, having a classroom library gives children instant access to books and other print materials. Taking children to attend the school's main library and/or a public library regularly, and helping them get library cards, assures that children can update their print collections on an ongoing basis, and may encourage them to develop the life-long habit of learning through reading. Young children are observed frequently pretending to read in comfortable library environments: they remember certain words from their favorite stories by using visual cues. This pretend reading can show children's considerable knowledge regarding the purposes of reading and its global characteristics.

Skills and activities that are important for kindergarten students' acquisition of reading and writing

Many children know something about the ABCs when they start kindergarten. It is important for kindergarten teachers to build on this knowledge by helping them to gain fluency in easily identifying and differentiating among letter shapes. Research has established well that kindergarteners' letter-naming proficiency is highly predictive of their achievement at the end of the year, likely due to its mediation of memory for sounds. Learning theorists recommend beginning with the upper-case letters that are visually the easiest, and progressing to lower-case letters. They also find that mastery is facilitated, not by introducing many letters at once, but by introducing only a few at a time. Developmentally, children's ability to name letters easily coincides with their ability to associate letters with speech sounds. However, phonemic awareness also requires practice and time to develop fully. Kindergarteners with good phonemic awareness can identify rhyming and non-rhyming words, and words with the same initial or final sounds; they can segment short words into individual phonemes, and blend phonemes into words

Importance of the alphabetic principle to effective reading instruction

For children to succeed in the first and subsequent grades, they must understand sound-to-letter correspondences, as well as having phonemic awareness and letter knowledge. They must know phonics in order to identify words accurately and fluently. Overall successful reading, even at older ages, depends in large part on the ability to read words. Poor readers are likely to rely on the surrounding context to decipher new words; good readers use their decoding skills, name new words, and then, associate meaning with them. They only use context for assistance in figuring out a new word's meaning once they have decoded it. These decoding skills are also important to beginning readers for facilitating fluency and automaticity in reading. Students who read fluently (i.e. quickly and easily) are far more likely to have good reading comprehension. Therefore, providing material at the student's Independent level—i.e. s/he needs no assistance and achieves 95% word accuracy—is important. Some poor readers have learned fundamental phonics but still have specific difficulties with automatic, fluent reading.

Aspects of the interrelationship of children's reading and writing

Reading and writing are inextricable; some educators call them, "two sides of the same coin" (Learning First Alliance, 2000). Just as we cannot speak intelligibly without being able to listen to spoken language, we cannot write without being able to read. Reading and writing are both dependent on fluent comprehension and application of language on multiple levels. Reading and writing reciprocally benefit one another. Beginning in first grade (or sooner), children are afforded daily occasions for organizing their thoughts, transcribing, and editing them by writing. Experts recommend teachers provide writing assignments that both fit student ability levels and vary in nature. Teachers should assign both expository and narrative writing, for instance. While children are developing skills in forming letters, spelling words, and generating sentences, teachers should also teach them the stages of composition. First they can work as partners or groups to produce and organize ideas. Then they can create drafts; share ideas with peers for feedback; and, successively, learn and practice revision, editing, proofreading, and publishing.

Relationship of handwriting and spelling to instructional plans for student success with written composition

Researchers have found that in the same way that fluency in recognizing words supports reading comprehension, mastery of handwriting and spelling skills supports written composition. Students who learn to form letters accurately and fluently and spell words correctly and easily write better-organized, lengthier compositions. Teachers must instruct students concurrently in composition strategies—such as identifying main ideas; writing topic sentences, introductions and conclusions; paragraphing appropriately, etc.—and in the required writing conventions, such as spelling, handwriting, capitalization, punctuation, and word usage. Explicit instruction in spelling and handwriting skills from first grade on, and frequent assignment of purposeful writing applying these skills enable students to learn them more easily. Effective teachers stimulate students' appreciation and enthusiasm for reading and writing. Research finds children read to frequently and encouraged to enjoy books and read extensively have better chances of becoming good readers. In addition to teaching specific literacy skills, selecting varied reading materials, using libraries, integrating literacy across the curriculum, and continual school initiatives promoting love of books and reading strengthen literacy instruction.

Conditions that are required for a student to learn to read

(1) Phonological awareness is recognizing the sound structures of spoken language, not just the meanings it conveys. This is a reading prerequisite. (2) Phonemic awareness is the skill of recognizing and manipulating individual speech sounds or phonemes. Students must be able to segment words and syllables into phonemes to learn to read. (3) The Alphabetic Principle is the concept that printed language consists of alphabet letters that are deliberately and systematically related to the individual sounds of spoken language. Reading depends on understanding this concept. (4) Orthographic awareness is recognition of printed language structures, such as orthographic rules, patterns in spelling; derivational morphology and inflectional morphology, i.e. structural changes indicating word types and grammatical differences; and etymology, i.e. word and meaning origins. Efficient reading requires orthographic awareness. (5) Comprehensive monitoring strategies: Students need full repertoires of techniques that will help them to attend to and retain the information that they read.

Fundamental skills that students must know to learn to read well

To become good readers, students must have phonological awareness, i.e. knowing the structures of speech sounds. They must understand the alphabetic principle, i.e. that alphabet letters represent specific speech sounds in print and writing. They must have orthographic awareness, i.e. knowing the rules, structures, and patterns in the spelling and grammar of written/printed language. And they must have acquired multiple and varied strategies to support their reading comprehension and retention. Teachers must be educated and prepared in linguistics, psycholinguistics, and reading; in how to assess and diagnose student skills in reading and spelling; and in a thorough complement of strategies for conducting reading interventions. Teachers need to instruct their students in such concepts and skills as segmenting words/syllables; alliteration; rhyming; phonics patterns and their representation in text; conventions of spelling and writing; being able to identify the main idea in text; being able to draw inferences from reading; and a wide range of study skills to help students comprehend, remember, and apply what they read.

Fundamental phonological awareness skills that young children must acquire

Young children must understand the idea of a separate word in spoken language before they enter kindergarten. Evidence of having acquired this skill is demonstrated when a child can identify single words within a spoken sentence. Children must also acquire the skill of recognizing and using rhymes. They should be able to identify a rhyme in words or syllables before they begin kindergarten. Given one word or syllable, they should be able to complete a rhyme with another word or syllable by the time they are in kindergarten. They should also be able to produce their own rhyme(s) during kindergarten. Children must be able to manipulate syllables of words. By the time they are in kindergarten, children should be able to combine (blend) syllables into words; separate (segment) the syllables in a word; and delete syllables from words.

Skills of phonological awareness involving phonemes

Phonemes are separate speech sounds, including vowels and consonants. Children who are in kindergarten should be able to recognize the first and last phonemes of words, such as the /s/ and the /t/ in *sit*. By the first grade, students should be able to combine (blend) the initial phonemes of words with the stems of the words (such as the /s/ with [it] in *sit*). They should also be able to combine individual phonemes into syllables and words by first grade. First-grade students should be able to separate (segment) the phonemes in words. They should be able to remove the first phoneme from a word or syllable, and remove the last phoneme from a word or syllable. In addition, a student in first grade should be able to add a phoneme to a word or syllable. By the second grade, students should be able to remove phonemes from blends of several phonemes. They should also be able to substitute one phoneme for another in a word or syllable by the second grade.

Multisensory strategies that help first-grade students with phonological processing

Studies show phonological processing deficits are the most frequent obstacles to young students acquiring early reading skills. Multisensory procedures incorporate vision, hearing, touch, and movement. Via visual, auditory, tactile, and kinesthetic sensory modalities, children process speech sounds and phonemes through varied channels. This helps them understand and remember phonemes. Multisensory mapping helps emergent or struggling readers, or those with learning disabilities. However, this activity should be used to supplement instruction, not to introduce phonemic awareness. Teachers and students can sing or chant a song or poem together while teachers highlight keywords. Then they read aloud together. Teachers identify targeted phonemes in the material, asking students to match each with a picture by sorting picture cards. Teachers have students chant each phoneme, simultaneously "writing" the corresponding letter in the air. Teachers have students trace each letter in sand or cornmeal while saying the corresponding phoneme, immediately followed by generating words starting or ending with it. To review, teachers supply letter cards with bumpy or textured surfaces and pictures to paired students to repeat the procedure with prior and new phonemes and letters.

Instructional strategy for generating rhymes

Teachers can use a rhyme-generating strategy with monosyllabic words for kindergarten students and with multisyllabic words for older students. Teachers first introduce the concept of rhyming, asking students for definitions and examples of rhymes. Then the teachers read a rhyming poem or song lyrics aloud to the students, asking them to identify which of the words rhyme. Teachers chart these words for students, color-coding the onset (word-initial phoneme) and rime (word-stem) of each rhyming word. Teachers use a word ladder graphic to show students how they can use existing words to generate new word stems (rimes). Teachers chart word-initial consonants and show students how to change (manipulate) these to make new rhymes. For example, *fat-cat-sat-mat*. The teacher selects sentences from the poems or song that are read aloud and writes them on strips of paper ("sentence strips"). The teacher then has students generate new rhymes by producing sentences of their own to fit the poem or song context. Teachers also develop student manipulation skills by having them generate rhymes with their own and classmates' names.

Instructional activity using picture cards

Phonemic awareness can be difficult for young children because phonemes are abstract concepts, but related activities demand they manipulate them like concrete objects. Explicit training in phonemic recognition and manipulation is found by researchers to promote children's skills in phonetic spelling and reading at significantly younger ages. Teachers can use picture cards with small groups or tutoring interventions to give children explicit, repetitive practice by matching pictures with word-initial, word-medial, or word-final phonemes. This technique incorporates graduated levels of scaffolding (support), differentiated target phoneme positions, and differentiated feedback, which teachers determine based on student assessment results. Teachers specifically model: target phonemes first, then drawing picture cards and matching them in a game format. Students then copy the model and the first student who identifies and matches a newly drawn card to the first card drawn gets the entire stack. Once this activity is complete, teachers help students review by having each student identify his or her matches.

Metalinguistic awareness

Metalinguistic awareness is the understanding that language is something we study. When young students have not made the connection that phonemes can be manipulated as objects, sound-sorting can help them realize that spoken words consist of separate sounds. Studies show activities identifying and classifying phonemes' word positions develop young readers' word-decoding and encoding skills. Teachers introduce a targeted phoneme in a musical chant, which students join. Teachers then model sorting the targeted sound; for example, *cat, sit,* and *bet* all end with /t/. They show students how to sort picture cards, grouping cards whose words all end with /t/. They have students explain why a selected card does not fit into the group. They assign paired students to sort picture cards into groups having the targeted sound in word-initial, word-medial, or word-final position. Students report and explain how they sorted and classified the cards. Teachers have students generate additional words fitting each category. The teachers write these words on charts, having students read them aloud to summarize the activity.

Blending and segmenting phonemes

Research from the National Reading Panel (2000) finds that instruction in phonological awareness is most effective when focused specifically on only one or two skills at a time within a lesson or activity. Also, practicing separating and combining phonemes prepares young students to decode and encode words for reading and writing. After modeling for and supporting first-grade students in segmenting and blending phonemes, teachers can implement a sound-play activity like "Treasure Chest." Teachers pair students according to their similar assessment results. They use a "Treasure Chest" sheet or board, pennies, and picture cards. Teachers name each picture card for students first. Each student pair draws a picture card, and one partner says its word and puts a penny into each box on the Treasure Chest for each sound in the word. The other partner combines the phonemes, says the word, and picks up the pennies. The partners then trade roles with a new set of picture cards.

Alphabetic principle and its relationship to student proficiency

A multitude of research has demonstrated that student efficiency and accuracy in reading depends in large part upon their knowledge of letter-sound correspondences. Studies have revealed that good readers see every letter in a word but, at the same time, their processing of whole words is rapid and automatic in nature. Therefore, students must not only understand the alphabetic principle to read well, they must also apply it fluently to be able to concentrate on the text's meaning. Not only struggling readers, but the majority of young students need systematic, explicit instruction to master and apply alphabetic principle skills. To read alphabetic printed language, students must have good word-decoding skills. For these, educators must provide explicit instruction in phonemes, in the reading of both regular and irregular words, and in reading connected text. This instruction needs to start in kindergarten. For most students, it must continue throughout the elementary grades. As texts increase in complexity, educators must also teach more advanced skills in word analysis to students.

Findings of evidence-based research into phonics instruction

Knowing the alphabetic principle is crucial to reading for decoding isolated words and connected text. Directly teaching a clear sequence of letter-sound correspondences, including both vowels and consonants, is characteristic of systematically teaching phonics. Research finds systematic instruction more effective than non-systematic teaching. Elementary school students show significant improvements in word identification, spelling, and reading comprehension from systematic, explicit phonics instruction. Research studies also find this type of instruction to be more effective for students from diverse economic, social, and cultural backgrounds, who make greater progress in reading than they do with no instruction or non-systematic and/or non-explicit instruction in phonics. Explicit and systematic phonics instruction is especially helpful for children having trouble learning to read. This kind of instruction is most beneficial when schools start it early, in kindergarten and first grade. Most students can complete phonics learning within two years—kindergarten through first grade, or first through second grade.

Basic elements of effective teaching

For instruction to be effective, teachers must model new skills for students so they can see demonstrations of concepts and actions that are unfamiliar to them. Teachers must provide multiple examples of all new tasks that they teach: students need variety, redundancy, and repetition to grasp the new concepts. Teachers must engage students during instructional activities. Simply lecturing or dictating a lesson will neither interest nor motivate students; they must be directly involved in learning activities. Teachers must encourage students for their efforts, not only for correct responses. Most early learners are unlikely to get everything right immediately or they would not need instruction. Without positive reinforcement, they will easily become discouraged, frustrated, lose interest and become less likely to participate. Teachers must give students immediate feedback for students to associate it with their immediately preceding response. They must also give immediate error correction for the same reason, and to ensure solid learning of correct responses. When teachers combine these elements with robust curricula, students learn more and learn better.

Research results regarding the benefits of teaching phonics explicitly and systematically

Numerous research studies have demonstrated that systematic instruction in phonics is superior to non-systematic instruction or no instruction in phonics for ensuring young students' development of reading skills, and that explicit instruction in phonics is likewise more effective than implicit, embedded, or incidental instruction in phonics. Explicit and systematic phonics instruction can reduce or eliminate the risk of developing reading problems in the future for young students who are experiencing problems in learning to read. Teachers can employ such systematic and explicit phonics instruction to individual students, small groups, or whole classes and have it be equally effective. However, while phonics is essential to early reading programs, it does not comprise a complete reading program. Beginning readers need more than phonics instruction: reading programs should also include consolidating alphabetic knowledge; participating in phonemic awareness activities; listening to informational books and stories that parents and teachers read aloud to them; and regularly reading and writing words, messages, letters, and stories.

Example of whole-class phonics instruction for kindergarten students

In the first week of a one-month unit among units over the school year, the Wright Group's LEAD21 model features these elements: On the first and third days, teachers introduce a skill to the class, such as segmenting the phonemes in words, and review it on the second and fourth days. On the fifth day, teachers work with students on discrimination, review, and additional practice of the skill. Every day begins with a warm-up in phonemic awareness. On the first and third days, for example, classes practice segmenting words into their component phonemes, use alphabet-sound cards, connect sounds to the letters that represent them, practice this connection, and practice writing letters. On the third day, students may use per-decodable or decodable readers to supplement their practice with phoneme segmentation and sound-to-letter correspondences. On the second and fourth days, students review sound-letter connections, review the writing of letters, and practice writing letters using high-frequency (most used) words.

Phonics and spelling are connected

Many research studies clearly demonstrate that phonics, spelling, and reading have a reciprocal and interactive relationship. According to the National Reading Panel, students improve their application of alphabetic knowledge to spelling via phonics instruction. When they spell words, students must encode them. In encoding, they apply sound-to-symbol relationships at higher levels. This in turn makes their phonics knowledge deeper. Instructional models like LEAD21 (Wright Group, 2010-2013) align phonics with spelling. Thus the model's lessons in spelling adhere to the same skills sequence and range as are covered in its phonics instruction. Both progress in complexity from simplest to most difficult. Students participate in various phonics activities. For example, teachers lead students in a phonemic awareness warm-up activity containing the phonemes in that week's spelling list. Students read sentences containing words using the week's spelling pattern. They may also read decodable books, individually or in small groups, with the related phonics and spelling components. Then teachers give them a spelling pre-test to introduce the week's spelling list.

Phonics instruction for whole classes in first grade according to an explicit and systematic model that integrates spelling

The LEAD21 instructional model (Wright Group) is systematized so teachers introduce two new phonics elements weekly. Progress is cumulative, with new elements introduced on day one of the week and reviewed and reinforced on day four. New elements introduced on day three are reviewed and reinforced on day two of the next week. Students conduct inquiry projects on the last weekday. The last week of the month is devoted to reviewing, with no new elements being introduced. Spelling concepts are based on phonics components in every lesson. Students practice what they learned in the class lesson independently at literacy stations. For units that cover phoneme blending, for example, teachers provide students with materials including sound-spelling cards and decodable readers. Teachers introduce and model the skill and have students practice it on days one and three using high-frequency words while they review and practice blending, review word patterns, and work on word-building on days two and four.

Levels of student achievement in phonics instruction

The Wright Group's LEAD21 model of phonics instruction, which incorporates reading and spelling, allows for teaching whole classes, small groups, and independent practice by individual students. This model identifies four levels: Intensive (students needing the most help), Strategic (students needing extra support), Benchmark (students achieving at expected levels), and Advanced (students surpassing expected achievement). Teachers can more closely monitor how students in small groups apply the specific phonics skills taught and learned. They can more easily offer coaching and support when necessary. Small-group instruction in this model offers students a *"Phonics Companion"* for practice including writing; decodable readers, which incorporate higher-than-usual numbers of words that feature particular targeted phonics components; and Differentiated Readers, wherein students can isolate specific phonics components when they find them. Decodable readers afford students practice for sound-to-letter correspondences during actual reading experiences. Studies find these readers are associated with better overall phonics knowledge and reading achievement. They can be used in both small groups and independent individual practice.

Significance of fluency to student reading

Research shows strong positive correlation between high student scores in reading fluency and high student scores in reading comprehension. Therefore, educators find practice for attaining reading fluency to be important. However, experts advise having all students repeatedly read passages using the same recordings is not a practice method to address diverse student needs. Differentiating instruction is preferred. Teachers can easily locate fluency passages online designed for different reading levels. They should assess student fluency rates at the Instructional level, i.e., with 85 to 95 percent word accuracy in two-minute periods. Using these assessment results, teachers should divide students into small groups of four to seven apiece, based on similar fluency assessment scores and reading levels. An example of different assessed student fluency rates is as followed: Group 1 students read 150 words in two minutes below grade level, Group 2 reads 151-180 words in two minutes at grade level, Group 3 reads 181-210 words in two minutes below grade level, and Group 4 reads more than 210 words in two minutes at grade level.

Phonological features of English that students must know and understand in order to develop academic language

In order to utilize academic English, students must know sound-to-symbol correspondences. In English, some of these are not regular or logical, as when the [s] in *sugar* is pronounced /ʃ/ instead of /s/ as in other words, or the different pronunciations of the letters "*ough*" in *tough, though, through, thought,* and *bough,* which makes them difficult. As well as knowing the phonemes associated with English spellings, students also need to understand and correctly use intonational and stress patterns. These can differ for different forms from the same word root, such as in progress versus progressive, or Canada versus Canadian; words that are different parts of speech that are spelled the same but stressed differently, like the noun record versus the verb record; or different words with different meanings, spelled differently and pronounced phonemically the same but with different stress patterns, such as incite versus insight. Additionally, when learning academic words derived from other languages, students have to learn new spelling patterns and phonemic combinations, like the words *antebellum* from Latin, *psychology* from Greek, and *rapport* from French.

Development of Reading Comprehension

Status of American elementary school-aged children's reading proficiency

A substantial proportion of American children have been found not to read well. For example, the National Assessment of Educational Progress (NAEP) defines the "basic" level of reading proficiency as "...partial mastery of the prerequisite knowledge and skills that are fundamental for proficient work at each grade" (2009). The NAEP's 2009 Reading Report Card found that 33% of fourth-graders in America read below this "basic" level. Many beginning kindergarteners are below grade level and/or behind their peers, and continue to be behind in successive grades. Variations in children's personal, familial, cultural, and socioeconomic backgrounds, life experiences, and exposure to print differentially affect their reading abilities, especially as upper school grades present more challenging reading matter. Research identifies these differences by ages of 3 years. Students with sufficient prior knowledge attain good reading comprehension, while those without it do not. The NAEP finds that proportionally more impoverished, black, and Hispanic students score below "basic" levels on its reading test than their age peers.

Respective importance of vocabulary and comprehension to effective instructional plans

The wider children's experience is with reading, the greater their acquisition of word knowledge, which is crucial for reading comprehension. School-aged children are required to learn thousands of new word meanings each year, the majority attained by hearing words read aloud and/or reading words in books themselves. The basis of rich, productive vocabulary is forming networks of conceptually-related words. To establish this foundation, children must actively process word meanings; this develops their comprehension of words, connections among word concepts, and word uses. Solid background knowledge and a large working vocabulary enable text comprehension. Even before children can read independently, teachers can provide instruction in comprehension through reading interactively and often with children from diverse expository and narrative texts. They should select texts that build on students' existing knowledge of the world. When teachers ask questions and invite student questions and discussions to confirm understanding, they improve students' text comprehension. Students are supported by effective instruction in relating textual concepts to their own experience/knowledge, and then retaining these ideas.

Teaching students to self-monitor their own reading comprehension

Educational researchers find that most students need explicit instruction that is intensive and given consistently, repeatedly, and over time in order to become good readers. Teachers select strategies that closely fit with the text they assign students to read. By "thinking aloud" and modeling, teachers describe and demonstrate each strategy and its importance. They guide students to learn when, where, and how to apply strategies; and they provide opportunities for students to apply them independently. After modeling, teachers guide students to practice deciding when and how to use strategies independently, giving them feedback and starting discussions. Teachers also have students independently apply the same strategies to other texts in later lessons. To enhance self-monitoring, teachers model for students how to: plan and clarify beforehand their reading's purpose/goal; consider their existing knowledge before and during reading; know whether they comprehend the text; apply strategies for deciphering hard words and concepts; question whether text makes sense; and discern how texts are organized. Teachers provide scaffolding/support that they gradually withdraw as students develop independence.

Behaviors to observe in students that show they are self-monitoring

As teachers, we must monitor whether students self-monitor during reading and how much: lack of self-monitoring undermines comprehension. Young children/early readers should self-monitor for 1:1 matching in beginning pattern books. They may use their fingers to help match print to sound. Early readers must monitor that the words they read look and sound right and make sense, learning to cross-check multiple information sources. All ages of students must self-monitor for punctuation cues to comprehend sentence meanings. Students must also self-monitor their pacing, phrasing, and fluency. Teachers can remind them if their reading sounds choppy to themselves, they should go back and realign elements to be smoother. Students reading longer texts self-monitor whether they are following the plot, distinguishing among characters, keeping track of settings, narrators, etc. With non-fiction, students should automatically ask themselves whether they understand it; whether the information is new to them; which parts seem more or less important; and check the context for meanings of unfamiliar (especially if bold-faced) words.

Expository text and narrative text

Expository text is text that is factual. It provides information, rather than telling a story as narrative text does. The main purpose of exposition is to inform the reader, explain something, or persuade the reader. Some examples include academic textbooks, journals, magazines, catalogues, brochures, diaries, and generally newspapers, biographies and autobiographies (some of these latter three may use narrative structure, but many use expository form). Throughout school especially, and also throughout life, students will read mostly expository text. To comprehend exposition, students must understand how the text is organized. Exposition lacks the storyline of narrative to guide their reading. Students must learn that authors use various structures to organize their thoughts in expository writing, such as comparison and contrast, time sequences and order sequences, cause-and-effect relationships, and patterns of problems-solutions. In a given text, section, or chapter, authors can employ several or all of these structures. Exposition can also be presented differently than narrative: headings and subheadings may organize it; graphics such as diagrams, tables, charts and illustrations may be included.

Narrative text and story grammar

Simply put, narrative is text that tells a story. This can include fables, myths, tall tales, legends, folk tales, fantasy and science fiction, short stories, novels; even some news reports, biographies, autobiographies, etc. Narrative structure usually has a beginning, middle, and end; and clear story grammar, i.e. elements of the story, including plots, themes, settings, characters; a central conflict; and a conflict resolution. Assisting students in learning to recognize recurring story grammar/elements gives them a "story schema," i.e. a mental construct of what comprises a story. With new stories, students can apply this schema to predict what could happen as the story unfolds; to imagine the looks, sounds, and behaviors of characters and settings; and summarize events in the plots. Teachers can enhance comprehension and self-monitoring by: inviting students to relate narrative characters and events to their own life experiences; focusing class discussions on story grammar; having students compare the structures of different stories they have read; and creating story maps and/or other visual aids to support recalling particular elements.

Strategies that students need to learn in order to read expository text

Expository text does not have a plot or storyline and characters the way that narrative text does, so students will not be focusing on those elements. Instead, they must understand the structure of exposition to comprehend what they read. Teachers can help them monitor and direct their reading of exposition independently by teaching them the following strategies: (1) to "chunk" textual information by grouping related concepts; (2) to summarize a text's most important information, also by grouping related ideas; (3) to integrate the information in an expository text with their own established knowledge; (4) to apply the information in an expository text to situations in real life; (5) to interpret the graphics, such as figures, tables, and charts in a text, and to be able to construct their own graphics; (6) to synthesize (i.e. pull together) the information from various texts that they read; and (7) to develop and deliver class presentations about the subject matter in the text they read.

Student motivation

Student motivation is vital to both their reading enough and their comprehending what they read. Students' learning to read is significantly aided by motivation, as are higher student literacy levels. The broader a student's reading experiences, the greater his/her ability to understand a broadening variety of the kinds and difficulty levels of texts. Good readers read copiously, in school and independently, choosing diverse texts for various purposes, such as for information, learning, curiosity, and entertainment. To support student motivation, teachers can: give students daily opportunities to read both texts they choose and those teachers and peers recommend; frequently afford both student-led and teacher-led discussions of their reading; arrange cooperative learning groups to discuss their reading and help one another select the best strategies for each text; encourage students to read for learning about ideas and/or subjects they find meaningful; engage them actively in reading-related pursuits; encourage independent reading; and give them opportunities to select from among texts with various reading levels and genres.

Directed Reading and thinking Activity (DRTA)

The DRTA (Stauffer, 1975) emphasizes reading as a process of thinking. It does this through its goal of teaching students to make predictions continually as they read narrative texts. While students are reading, the teacher interrupts them at selected, strategic spots in the story and asks them to predict what they think will happen next. The teacher also asks the students to confirm, reject, or change the story purposes they identified and the predictions they made. After students are done reading, the teacher asks the students to find any part(s) of the text that support what they predicted, and to read these aloud. They also require students to use the text itself to explain their own reasoning; and to supply proof that the students' predictions were correct or incorrect. Teachers may instruct the students to use charts for recording what they predict, and corresponding information they find in the text that proves or supports the accuracy of their predictions.

Reciprocal Teaching

Reciprocal Teaching (Palincsar and Brown, 1984) is described as a dialogue between teacher and students, wherein each member of the dialogue responds to the other. The class or group is reading a chosen text, and the teacher-student dialogue will focus on some portion of that text. The dialogue is organized by the application of four strategies for reading comprehension: (1) asking questions; (2) clarifying challenging ideas and words; (3) summarizing the material that the students have read; and (4) predicting what might occur next. Questioning, clarifying, summarizing, and predicting are examples of critical thinking in reading. First, the teacher models application of a comprehension strategy for the students, explaining this process. The teacher gradually transfers this activity to the students. Commensurately with their growing proficiency, the teacher increases the challenge levels of student participation. This helps students to recognize the benefits of applying comprehension strategies in real-life reading activities. It also helps teachers identify individual student problems in applying these strategies, and give individualized instruction to meet student needs.

Transactional Strategy Instruction (TSI)

Transactional Strategy Instruction (Brown and Coy-Ogan, 1993) is an instructional procedure that teaches students to use effective comprehension strategies to construct meaning from the text they read. It supports students in completing the following tasks: (1) planning and setting goals for reading; (2) activating their background knowledge and using textual cues to construct meaning from the text as they read; (3) self-monitoring their reading comprehension; (4) solving problems they experience while reading; and (5) self-evaluating their progress. To achieve these, teachers using TSI instruct them in applying reading strategies, which usually include the following: making predictions based on activating their previous knowledge; generating questions and asking them; clarifying where needed; visualizing the content that they read; relating the content in the text they read to their own existing background knowledge and experience; and summarizing what they have read. TSI is practiced in small groups, using these strategies to organize discussion of text, as students read orally and exchange their individual responses to and interpretations of the reading

Question-Answer Relationship (QAR)

Giving students questions, and/or helping students to formulate questions, to answer when they are reading provides students with purposes for their reading. Answering questions directs students' attention to focus on what they will learn from their reading; it encourages students' active thinking while they are reading; it prompts students to self-monitor their own reading comprehension as they read; and it supports students in reviewing the information they read and relating it to their existing knowledge. The QAR strategy helps students learn to improve their ability to answer questions about their reading. QAR asks students to classify the information they use to answer questions about their reading as explicit, i.e. it is directly stated in the text; implicit, i.e. it is implied in the text; it is derived completely from their own prior knowledge; or it is some combination of these.

General nature and benefits of reading comprehension strategies

Strategies for reading comprehension do not begin as automatic or intuitive practices; they are, rather, consciously developed plans that good readers employ for understanding the text they read. These plans consist of series of steps that readers apply to make sense out of their reading. When teachers give students instruction in reading comprehension strategies, this assists the students in developing control over their own understanding of the reading and developing into active, purposeful readers. One key strategy that students can use is to develop skill at monitoring their own reading comprehension. One component of monitoring is recognizing whether one understands something one reads or not. Another monitoring component is having identified and developed strategies to address comprehension problems as they occur. Research finds that even beginner reading students can improve their self-monitoring of comprehension with instruction. With such instruction, students learn to differentiate clearly what they do and do not understand, and to apply suitable strategies to address comprehension difficulties.

Graphic organizers

Graphs, charts, diagrams, maps, frames, webs, and clusters are all types of graphic organizers. They illustrate visually the concepts in a text and/or relationships among concepts. They benefit readers by helping them focus on particular ideas/concepts, and on how these are related to and interact with other ideas/concepts. Graphic organizers are tools that students can use to explore and demonstrate the relationships in a text. They can help students to focus on structural differences in texts as they read them; for example, between fictional and non-fictional writing. They also help students to compose organized summaries of text they read. Venn diagrams help students compare/contrast information from two books. Chain-of-events/storyboards help students order text events/steps in correct sequences. Story maps help students chart fictional narrative structures, e.g., identify settings, characters, events, problems, and resolutions; or identify main ideas and details as non-fictional expository structures. Cause-and-effect graphics help students visualize antecedents and consequences.

Questions that students can answer as part of a reading comprehension strategy

Answering questions about the text they are reading can help students understand it better. Four kinds of questions are: (1) "Right There" questions exist in the text, requiring one correct answer found in one place, such as a sentence/word. For example (using Arnold Lobel's Frog and Toad I Can Read Books series): "Who was Frog's friend?" Answer: "Toad." (2) "Think and Search" questions require recalling information located directly in the text, usually in multiple places. Students must think about and search through the passage for the answer. For example: "Why was Frog sad?" Answer: "Because his friend left." (3) "Author and You" questions ask students to comprehend text and relate it to their prior knowledge. For example: "What do you think Frog felt, seeing Toad again?" Answer: "Happy; I'm happy to see my friend who lives far away." (4) "On Your Own" questions require students' previous experiences and knowledge more than text. For example: "How would you feel if your best friend moved away?" Answer: "Sad; I'd miss him/her."

Generating questions, recognizing story structure, and summarizing text

When students must generate questions about what they read, they realize whether they understand it and whether they can answer their own questions. They learn to ask themselves questions requiring that they synthesize content from different portions of the text, such as questions about the text's main ideas and its important information. When students are taught to recognize content categories such as settings, characters, events, problems and resolutions in narratives, they learn to recognize story structure, frequently aided by story maps; this enhances their reading comprehension. Instruction in summarizing what they have read teaches students to discern what is important in the text they read, and to be able to express the important content in their own words. When they learn through such instruction to summarize their reading, students are better able to identify its main ideas, and to connect these; to generate central ideas from their reading; to avoid or delete superfluous information; and to remember what they have read.

Verbal rehearsal, the keyword method, and visualization

Verbal rehearsal is a behavior we all use to maintain information in our working memory and/or short-term memory; for example, we look up a phone number, and then repeat it aloud, sotto voce, or silently, continually until we dial it. Students can use verbal rehearsal to learn, remember, and apply small amounts of information within a limited time period. The keyword method is a strategy of visualizing pictures that can help students learn new vocabulary and new concepts. Students construct a mental picture of anything/everything that helps them remember—an image of the thing they want to remember, an image of the printed word for it—whatever works for each student. The keyword method is one form of visualization that focuses on a key word to remember. Visualization in general is creating a visual mental picture of a concept, which could be a word, numbers, a formula, or a visual image without verbal or numerical symbols.

Multipass learning strategy

The Multipass Strategy (Schumaker et al, 1982) was researched with students having learning disabilities (LD) and found to improve reading comprehension by helping students glean more information from printed text. It has three main parts: the Survey pass; the Size-Up or Textual Cues pass; and the Sort-Out pass. In one step of the Survey pass, students read the chapter's title, consider how it fits with previous chapters, and predict what this reading will cover. In another step, students read the table of contents and decide how this chapter/portion is related to earlier parts. In another step, students read the chapter's introduction and identify the main idea. In another step, students skip to the end of the reading portion or chapter, read the summary, and compose a summary statement. Another step requires students to determine how the chapter is organized by reading its subtitles and other organizational elements, and then write an outline in their own words based on the main headings in the chapter.

Multipass is a learning strategy designed by researchers (Schumaker et al, 1982) to help teenage students with learning disabilities (LD) related to reading. It consists of an initial Survey pass, a medial Size-Up pass, and a final Sort-Out pass. In the second or Size-Up pass, students look for textual cues to aid their comprehension of the text. They review the illustrations (drawings/paintings, maps, graphs, charts, diagrams, etc.) and consider why these are included in the chapter. Then they read the questions provided at the beginning of the chapter, throughout it, and at the end. They mark any questions they can answer at the time. Then students read through the vocabulary words noted in the chapter. After this, they reread the headings within the chapter, which they had reviewed during the initial pass. They ask themselves questions based on the chapter's textual cues, and scan the selection for answers. When they find answers to the questions, they paraphrase them (restate them in their own words).

The Multipass learning strategy (Schumaker et al, 1982) is designed to help students, particularly those in high school who have reading disabilities, to improve their reading comprehension by following steps to access more of the meaning from the text they are reading. They make three passes of a text chapter: One to survey the chapter's title, introduction, table of contents, subtitles, and summary; another to "Size Up" the selection by analyzing textual cues such as illustrations, study questions, vocabulary words; and by reviewing the headings again, generating questions based on them, finding the answers by scanning the chapter, and paraphrasing this information. In the third "Sort-Out" pass, students read each study question provided on the chapter. They then try to answer every question. They mark those they were able to answer. For those they do not know, they scan the outlines they made based on chapter headings in the initial pass to find answers, repeating their scans as needed until they have answered all questions.

Academic vocabulary that students will need to read increasingly complex texts

Since common core standards have been created for all U.S. states and adopted by most of them, the emphasis in teaching academic vocabulary is shifting, from teaching literary terms (e.g., alliteration or onomatopoeia) that are less practical for content-area literacy and literacy across the curriculum, to teaching more commonly occurring and essential words (e.g., theory, principled, generation, and discourse). As textbooks become more and more complex with ascending grade levels, students must have general skills to be able to read and comprehend them across the various content area disciplines. To do this, students will need to build their databases of vocabulary reflecting words that are powerful across academic and workplace disciplines. They will also need to use such "language of power" words across content areas in speech and writing. To facilitate these student tasks, teachers must develop student abilities for accessing and using words; strategically focus on the most critical, prevalent new vocabulary words; concentrate on words students will use most; and teach students fewer words, but more in-depth.

Information genre of written text

Information books are books whose main intent is to report facts about the nature of a certain thing, such as weather or rocks; or of a particular genus or species of plant or animal. Four required elements of the information genre are: (1) topic presentation; (2) descriptive attributes; (3) characteristic events, describing typical processes, events, or actions that the topic is engaged in or does; and (4) final summary. Eight additional elements, which are optional rather than required, are (1) a prelude; (2) comparison(s) of different categories, types, or instances of the topic; (3) historical vignette(s); (4) experimental idea(s); (5) an afterword; (6) addenda; (7) a recapitulation; and (8) illustration extension(s). In addition, the information genre has certain features. These include a table of contents; headings; diagrams; pictures and photographs; captions; the use of a technical vocabulary; the use of generic nouns; the use of the timeless present tense; a glossary of terms; and an index.

Combined text genre of books

Traditionally, two major genres of books have been narrative, i.e. stories, and expository, i.e. informational. The combined-text genre, however, uses a combination of narrative and expository formats within one book. In the Magic School Bus series, for instance, fantasy stories like a class field trip to the ocean floor (Cole, 1992) are combined with information like reference charts and reports included in illustrations of the classroom. In Snowflake Bentley (Martin, 1998), the biography of Bentley is narrative; the specialized photography technique he developed is explained through informational margin notes. Stellaluna (Cannon, 1993) tells a fantasy narrative, followed by informational text about the characters' real-life equivalents. Cook-a-Doodle-Doo! (Stevens & Crummel, 1999) integrates exposition about using cookbooks and cooking with narrative about farm animals making strawberry shortcake. Both students and teachers can become distracted by multiple concepts and overwhelmed about navigating contrasting formats; elementary students cannot differentiate fantasy from scientific concepts. The solution, which also makes reading most effective, is to read these books in layers: illustrations; information; narrative; and additional details.

Using combined-text books

Combined-text books, incorporating narrative and informational formats within the same book, can expand student knowledge bases about diverse topics, also giving students experience applying this knowledge to fictional/fantasy stories. Teachers should closely observe concepts shared between both formats. Then, using various strategies during reading, rereading, and reviewing a book, teachers can improve student abilities to develop concepts, facts, and stories simultaneously. Experts recommend (1) reading the Illustrations layer, using a picture walk before reading to activate and/or develop schemata and stimulate student questions and comments on the informational topic; and the Pre-Reading Plan (PReP) to elicit and address student questions or misconceptions. (2) Reading the informational layer can be facilitated using the "zoom in, zoom out" strategy to identify salient concepts; and concept of definition (CD) maps to help students recognize concept interrelationships and levels. (3) Reading the narrative layer is aided by interactive read-alouds and creating story maps. (4) Reading the additional details layer, e.g., sketches and page borders, is supported by semantic maps and shared writing exercises.

Developing interdisciplinary units or writing across the curriculum has historically required combining narrative, informational, and pictorial texts into text sets on a specific topic. An advantage of combined-text books is that teachers can use them as focal texts to connect other books to the topic. For example, teachers can use other books in the text set throughout their unit, and a combined-text book for read-alouds. Using strategies appropriate to each layer of a combined-text book will inform students of the purposes of reading specific texts, and show them how strategic reading builds on their existing areas of concept knowledge. Teaching layers with associated strategies also helps students and teachers more easily identify target, superordinate, coordinate, and subordinate concepts. Clear identification of these helps teachers utilize materials optimally to meet state and national educational standards. Individual read-alouds for each layer allow teachers to model revisiting text for different purposes. Students more easily develop teacher-targeted concepts through reading individual layers, and establish fundamental knowledge for recognizing and differentiating fact from fantasy.

Illustrations in informational children's books

Just as museum displays, educational TV shows and movies must balance factual information that interests viewers with visual effects that fascinate them, so too must informational children's books balance interesting facts with fascinating visual illustrations. In high-quality children's nonfiction, all of the illustrations should be large and clear, and not excessively "busy" or crowded. Including photographs is always an important part of nonfiction. Light-colored or white backgrounds help add contrast to photos to be more appealing to children. The illustrations should explain the book's content and enhance it. Also, any included captions and/or labels should be simple, and yet should also name or explain the illustrations sufficiently. A good example of watercolor illustrations that support the text is in Pallotta's (1987) The Bird Alphabet Book. Two examples of children's books that incorporate colorful photographs that reinforce their text content include Meharry's (2001) Mud, Mud, Mud and Cowley's (2005) Chameleon, Chameleon.

Organization of informational children's books

How children's books are organized can provide the same benefits to young readers as directing signs in buildings or road maps. Good organization guides readers through books, helping them alternate attention effortlessly between text and illustrations and browse interesting topics. An informational book should, when applicable, include a table of contents, glossary of terms/vocabulary words, and index. Divisions between sections should be clear; headings and subheadings should be included as needed. For younger children who read independently, a good example of a well-organized book is Reid & Chessen's (1998) Bugs, Bugs, Bugs! It clearly separates illustrations from text; identifies one insect body part per page; and closes with two pages of interesting facts about insects and a basic index. Another example, for older children to read independently and younger children to browse and learn facts or read with adults, is Adams' (2001) The Best Book of Volcanoes. It opens with a pictorial table of contents; clearly divides topics, subtopics, text, and illustrations; and includes an illustrated glossary and an index.

Typographical characteristics that quality children's informational books should include

When selecting information books for young readers, adults should appraise not only their covers, topics, content, illustrations, and organization, but also attributes like font size, type, placement, and spacing. For younger children, letters should be larger than for adults or older children, with a clear and simple type style. Smaller letters are hard for young children to read, and unusual lettering styles are distracting for beginning readers. Also, words, and spaces between letters and words, should be placed on the page to ensure optimal reading ease. For inexperienced readers, anything less straightforward will impede reading comprehension. Young readers should be able to follow text on each page without effort. Publishers have recently produced many informational book series with brief, simple content, which young readers can easily read on their own. The Scholastic Time to Discover series has these characteristics. For example, one of its titles, Berger and Berger's (2002) Ants, Bees, and Butterflies includes a large font, consistent letter placement and spacing, and an easy reading level.

Tier 1, 2 and 3 vocabulary words

Tier 1 words are those used in everyday conversation, like house or car. Tier 2 words are often used in mature language, less in everyday speech but more in writing. These can strongly affect verbal functioning and well adapted to teaching during read-aloud interactions. Tier 3 words are academic vocabulary, usually taught during content-area lessons. In vocabulary instruction, teacher focus levels include: (1) incidentally exposing students to new words; (2) embedding instruction in discussion; and (3) focusing instruction on vocabulary. To expose students incidentally to words, the teacher incorporates Tier 2 words into discussions of read-alouds; e.g., "He wanted to know; his curiosity got the better of him." In embedding instruction, the teacher gives a synonym to define a word, and points at the book's illustration of it, e.g., "He's using a stick, called an oar, [pointing] to move the boat." In focused instruction, the teacher might define "get set" as getting ready, leading a discussion with students giving examples of things they get set for, like holidays or school.

Incidental exposure, embedded instruction, and focused instruction

Before, during, and after a teacher reads a story aloud to the class, s/he uses incidental exposure by incorporating less familiar words in discussions and providing contextual clues to their meanings. For instance, the teacher might describe characters as "coming bearing gifts;" or as "humble." This instructional level builds vocabulary knowledge without direct instruction. When target vocabulary words are not central to the story, and/or they express concepts the students recognize, teachers use embedded instruction, giving information about the words' meanings via short definitions or synonyms, interrupting the reading-aloud flow as little as possible. When vocabulary words are essential to comprehending the story, and/or when students have trouble comprehending their meaning, teachers use focused instruction. This includes a wide range of teacher-student interactions, from 4-25 instances, and frequently occurs before or after reading. It may depend on keywords that teachers have identified; and/or it may consist of spontaneous teacher responses to students' confusion and/or questions during the reading.

Definitional, contextual, and conceptual types of vocabulary knowledge

A teacher's learning goal for his/her young students influences the characteristics of instructional activities using read-alouds and discussions. When the goal is just to expose students to a new word, and/or when students are familiar with a word's conceptual basis, teachers use the definitional approach—giving students a definitional phrase or a synonym for a word, or eliciting these from students. This is a time-efficient approach, permitting teachers to address many words during read-alouds. When teachers have students refer to the text to ascertain a word's meaning, they are developing students' contextual word knowledge. They may reread a word's sentence context to help students prove or disprove their ideas of its meaning. For students to develop in-depth word comprehension, learning definitions is usually insufficient; they need conceptual knowledge to connect new words with words they already know and with their previous experiences. Teachers develop concepts via examples and questioning before reading; reinforcing definitions during reading; and giving students opportunities to use new words in various other contexts.

Enhancing students' ability to learn vocabulary words during reading-aloud interactions

To optimize students' ability to learn new word meanings, experts recommend that teachers use the following steps, identified through research into effective teacher practices: (1) Before reading, identify words in the text that (a) are central to comprehension, (b) are Tier 2 words to build students' reading vocabulary, and (c) are interesting and/or fun to say; and target 4-5 words for teaching more in-depth comprehension. (2) Ascertain the kind of vocabulary learning needed: incidental, embedded, or focused instruction; before, during, or after reading; and strategies to apply, by identifying familiar words used in new ways; new words for familiar concepts; words expressing new/unfamiliar concepts; and words essential to comprehension. (3) Identify instructional strategies commensurate with learning goals—e.g., synonyms/gestures with new words for familiar terms; pre-reading questioning and examples to develop new concepts; simple definitions during reading to reinforce learning. (4) Prepare a "Plan B" if a strategy fails, e.g., giving clarifications, corrections, synonyms, examples, and simple definitions. (5) Incorporate new vocabulary words learned into other classroom contexts.

Importance of vocabulary development to student reading skills

For close to a century, researchers have recognized students' vocabulary learning as significantly predictive of their reading comprehension. More recently, research also finds general reading performance and school achievement highly predicted by vocabulary knowledge. Researchers have also noted that students' decoding skills are predicted by their receptive vocabulary development. Students who know more words can read and comprehend text more easily. However, students typically enter school with widely varying levels of vocabulary knowledge. This variation is increased by students' diverse socioeconomic backgrounds and/or cognitive capacities. Research finds such variance across school grades; therefore, without intervention, differences among students only increase, so lower-performing students find catching up with age/grade peers more difficult. Moreover, students with reading problems demonstrate greater comprehension gains through vocabulary instruction than students without reading problems. Thus, educational experts advise integrating vocabulary into daily literacy instruction as crucial. To improve reading comprehension, teaching vocabulary should include both word definitions and contexts; engage students in deep processing; and offer students multiple exposures to the same words.

Integrating progressively more sophisticated vocabulary words into a classroom routine

Researchers have described an effective fourth-grade teacher's use of a daily, morning greeting activity, which was not only important to her classroom management plan and to building the classroom community, but moreover provided engaging vocabulary-learning experiences. Each student would greet the classmate to his/her left using a positive descriptor. Students began with simple adjectives like "nice," "talented," and "happy." Over time, the teacher encouraged them to use more original synonyms, like "friendly," "creative," and "jolly." Eventually, the teacher modeled the greeting using more sophisticated synonyms, like "affable," "virtuous," and "jovial." These unfamiliar words motivated students to look them up in dictionaries to understand their meanings, which they then remembered through associating them with real classmates. This strategy also

- 33 -

motivated students to make greater efforts to use more sophisticated adjectives each time they performed the greeting activity. Students soon were comfortable using large descriptive lexicons; soon thereafter, the teacher observed them using these words in classroom discussions, casual conversations, and writing assignments, proving their word ownership, application, and generalization.

Four types of vocabulary

Educational researchers have defined vocabulary as oral, print, receptive, and productive. When children listen to speech—including being read aloud to—and produce speech, they understand and use oral vocabulary words. When they read and/or write, they use print vocabulary. When they are listening or reading, they are using receptive vocabulary. When they are speaking or writing, they are using productive vocabulary. Researchers find that students' productive vocabulary words are more familiar, better known, and used more often than are words in their receptive vocabularies. They also observe that children's receptive vocabularies are bigger than their productive vocabularies, and that receptive vocabulary is essential to children's early reading development. As children learn to decode printed words in texts, they apply their existing vocabulary knowledge to attain comprehension of what they are reading. Therefore, if words in the text they read are not included in their vocabularies, young readers will not understand the text. Thus it is crucial to develop children's early vocabularies for them to read with comprehension.

General nature of children's vocabulary development

Experts find children's word knowledge is not black-and-white, i.e. simply knowing/not knowing a word's meaning, but a continuum of how much a student knows about a word, from a little to a lot. One classification of vocabulary knowledge (Dale, 1965) has four levels: (1) never heard/saw the word before; (2) heard/saw the word but does not know its meaning; (3) recognizes the word within context as related to some concept/topic/meaning; and (4) knows the word well. Another classification (Beck et al, 1987) identifies five levels along the continuum: (1) no knowledge of the word; (2) general idea; (3) narrow, contextually-dependent knowledge; (4) some knowledge, but unable to retrieve the word for suitable applications; and (5) rich, context-independent knowledge of word meaning. While some researchers advocate deeper understanding of fewer words, to apply vocabulary learned during writing and speaking as well as reading; and others emphasize acquiring greater vocabulary breadth for comprehending diverse texts, the majority agree that both depth and breadth are important to children's word knowledge.

Researchers have found that typically, a third-grade student knows approximately 8,000 vocabulary words, while a typical high-school student knows 25,000-50,000 or more words. Most students learn 3,000-4,000 new words every year. Vocabulary instruction therefore is a giant undertaking, given the numbers of new words a student acquires annually. Four essential elements of vocabulary instruction (Graves, 2000) are (1) reading widely; (2) teaching individual words; (3) strategies for learning words; and (4) developing word consciousness. Word consciousness is defined as being aware of words and their meanings; being interested in these; being aware of how and when new vocabulary words are used; being motivated to learn new words, and being able to use newly learned words with skill. Across all grade and age levels, it is critical for teachers to support development of students' word consciousness, particularly in those students who have previously had limited exposure to sufficient volume, variety, breadth, and depth of vocabulary.

Promoting word consciousness in students

Students from backgrounds of economic poverty, in both rural and urban areas, and those who are English-language learners (ELLs), have fewer chances to learn English vocabulary words at home. However, effective teachers have developed word consciousness—including strong motivation to learn more new words—in these students. These teachers used such practices as providing word-rich environments and enabling students' success and enjoyment in learning new words throughout the curriculum and school year. Consequently, these students noticed unfamiliar words used by others and asked their meanings; and they identified new words they had learned when they heard them being used in various contexts, connecting them with other words and gaining deeper comprehension of the new words. Researchers find that such word consciousness strongly eases the challenge of students' learning thousands of new words annually—particularly because research also finds that a major agent of children's vocabulary growth is incidental, contextual learning, through unstructured situations like communicating orally and reading casually without direct instruction, as well as routine teacher modeling.

Impact of reading skills on student success

The ability to read is not simply one academic area; it is a basic skill set underlying all academic activity, and determines whether students fail or succeed in school. Research shows that of first-graders with poor reading skills, 88% still read poorly in fourth grade. By this time, most information that students require is provided in text form. For this reason, the focus shifts from learning to read in the earlier grades, to reading to learn by fourth grade. Consequently, students with poor reading skills can find it harder to access and interact with the content in their schools' curricula. Moreover, reading abilities that are delayed or disordered usually are identified in higher elementary grades. Yet research finds remediation attempts then could be too late, because children acquire language and have literacy experiences from birth. Phonemic awareness, the alphabetic principle, and print awareness normally develop in early childhood. Children missing such early experiences will fall behind peers without extra instruction. This means elementary school teachers must give these children literacy-rich environments

Using themes to connect texts used for shared reading exercises with texts used in other teaching/learning contexts

Any inclusive classroom will contain students who read at various age/grade levels. As a result, some books used as core texts are going to present difficulties for some of the students, who read below grade level and/or lack background knowledge and vocabulary of the subject. One way a teacher can facilitate all students' comprehension of such texts is to provide supplementary texts that allow readers at different levels easier access—texts on the same subject or theme as the more difficult core text. Teachers have students read these more accessible texts independently during small-group reading periods. This makes it easier for students with less reading proficiency to learn the core vocabulary and build their background knowledge. Thus they are more prepared to tackle the more difficult core text during whole-class shared reading periods. With such preparation, less proficient readers are more likely to become engaged and active participants in the shared reading of a difficult text in the whole-group setting.

Keeping a journal

By keeping a journal, a student can record such things as: the particular errors and/or kinds of errors s/he is making on any given day; the particular mistakes s/he corrected successfully that day; the specific successes s/he experienced with reading; how many new vocabulary words s/he has learned; the feelings, such as frustration, anger, sadness, inadequacy, s/he experiences when struggling with reading; and the feelings of control, happiness, excitement, mastery, and higher self-esteem and self-efficacy s/he experiences accompanying improvements in reading. Journal writing enables a student to reflect on his/her progress, both on a daily basis and over time. Similarly to the way a student can gain both insights and pride by reviewing his/her cumulative work products in a portfolio assessment, the student can reread his/her journal entries over a time period of time and realize his/her improvements. Journaling allows a student to increase self-corrections, and also to reflect on his/her reading behaviors—developing metacognition, i.e., thinking about thinking and understanding the nature of one's own thought and learning processes.

Supporting school-wide reading initiatives

To achieve leadership in school-wide initiatives focused on the reading curriculum, educators should first be knowledgeable in the criteria for choosing a robust core reading program. They should ensure that whatever reading program they pick is effective enough to help the majority of students achieve success. They should also be able to identify how their school reading program demonstrates the "five big ideas" of reading (phonemic awareness, the alphabetic principle, fluency with text, vocabulary, and comprehension). School leaders should help the school's staff to select intervention and supplemental programs that have been proven effective by research-based evidence. Leaders should also support the school staff in developing and applying CSI maps. CSI stands for Core, Supplemental, and Intervention programs. CSI maps are grade-level plans indicating which Core, Supplemental, and Intervention programs will be used in instruction; and for how many minutes per day these will be taught according to student instructional levels. Furthermore, school administrators and other non-teaching leaders should learn their curriculum as well as the teachers.

Stimulating student motivation to read

School leaders can increase students' motivation to read by visiting classrooms and reading to students, showing their and the school's commitment to reading, demonstrating its importance and enjoyment. They should visit classes during reading group activities, praising student successes. They can let students come to their offices to read. Leaders should read some of the same books their students are reading, and discuss the books with them. This not only shows students the leaders' interest in them and their interests; it also helps leaders learn about students' interests, opinions, and reading motivations. Leaders can use programs, such as Battle of the Books or Reading Counts, to stimulate student motivations for reading. Leaders can sponsor/expedite special events reading-related for students. They should periodically participate in student progress monitoring. On occasion, they can personally teach a small student group. They can present students with goals, challenging them to read to attain these. Leaders can also do some of their own reading in classrooms during silent reading periods, so students see them reading.

Professional development

In research into professional development, participating teachers identified two components that had the greatest influence on their skills and knowledge whereby they changed their teaching practices. An emphasis on content knowledge was the first component. The second was coherence; this entails building upon teachers' existing knowledge. A responsibility of effective professional development is to assist teachers in aligning their instructional content with the school district's and state's standards and assessment procedures. Teacher support from professional development coaches includes encouraging teachers to share with each other their reflections on how they apply the new information they learn to fortifying their teaching practices. Good professional development should provide teachers with information about scientific reading research evidence-based instructional programs, strategies, and materials. It should promote active teacher engagement in skills, planning, and information. Goals of professional development include enabling teachers to use assessment data to direct their teaching; and improving teacher abilities for implementing programs of early intervention and remediation in reading.

Experts recommend that high-quality professional development for educators include such activities as: collaboration among colleagues to analyze assessments and plan instruction at each grade level; collaboration among teachers of different content-area subjects, also for purposes of analyzing assessments and planning instruction; collaboration among specialists in different areas of education, for the same purposes as the previous two activities; modeling of effective instructional practices and behaviors; peer coaching among educators; vertical teaming (i.e. collaboration among colleagues who teaching different grade levels); the formation of book study groups; and the conduction of action research and the sharing of what that research finds. Professional development regarding school core programs typically occurs during summer so that teachers are prepared for the new school year. To prepare teachers for implementing their schools' selected core, supplemental, and intervention programs, professional development should also provide them with program-specific training. All personnel involved, not only teachers, should receive professional development, particularly for school-wide reading programs, because all participants are needed to coordinate objectives, training, and assessments.

Teaching reading comprehension skills to fifth-grade students

Comprehension skills and techniques can be taught to fifth-grade students in eight connected units, for example, with each unit covered over four weeks. In the second unit, the first week could teach the skill of differentiating facts from opinions in text. Students can learn the strategy of summarizing text they read. An associated text feature is captions in the text. In the second week, teachers reinforce the summarizing strategy and review how to tell facts from opinions. An associated text feature is the text's index. During the third week, teachers focus on instructing students in identifying main ideas and supporting details in text. They teach students the supporting strategy of making predictions about the text. Text features associated with this skill and strategy include the tone and mood of the writing in the text. In the fourth week of this unit, teachers should reinforce students' knowledge of the predicting strategy and review with them how to identify the main ideas and supporting details in a text.

Fifth-grade teachers can instruct their students in reading comprehension by using an eight-unit sequence, with each four-week unit covering one or two essential reading skills and one or two related reading strategies. In the fifth of eight units, for example, teachers can focus on the skill of sequencing events. They teach students the strategy of summarizing text to support this skill. They can use the associated text feature of sidebars. The second week, teachers review the sequencing skill by reviewing the summarizing strategy from the first week, using the text feature of line graphs to show sequences. The third week, teachers instruct students in skills of categorization and classification and teach the related strategy of making predictions, employing the literary element of the character. In the fourth week of this unit, teachers review with students the strategy of determining important information and the skill of classifying and categorizing what they taught them in previous units.

Teachers can follow a model of an eight-unit instructional sequence for fifth grade, wherein each unit comprises four weeks. In the fourth of eight units, teachers can focus on teaching students to identify cause-and-effect relationships in text. The first week of this unit, they can teach students the strategy of making connections between events to support learning this skill. A related text feature they can use is cutaways in the text. The second week, teachers reinforce the connection-making strategy, reviewing the cause-and-effect identification skill taught the first week by using the text feature of bulleted lists in text. The third week of this unit, teachers can work on developing students' skills for recalling and retelling what they read in a text, teaching them the supporting strategy of visualization by using the associated text feature of the author's message or theme. The fourth week of this unit, teachers reinforce the visualizing strategy and review the recalling and retelling skills they taught the previous week.

In the first week of a four-week unit in a reading comprehension instructional sequence, an example of a student skill is determining a text author's purpose. The associated strategy is to determine the important information in a text. An example of a text feature that teachers can focus on with students is a bar graph. In the second week of this unit, a review of determining the author's purpose is accompanied by reinforcing the strategy of determining the important information in the text. An associated text feature is a glossary of terms included in the text. During the third week, the skill of paraphrasing is supported through teaching the strategy of making inferences about text; an associated literary element is a plot featuring a problem and solution. In the fourth week of this unit, the skill of paraphrasing text is reviewed, and the strategy of drawing inferences from text is reinforced.

An instructional sequence in reading comprehension for fifth-graders can consist of eight units, for example, with classes focusing on a different skill in each four-week unit. As an example of the third of eight units, teachers can focus on teaching students the skill of comparing and contrasting. They teach students the related strategy of asking questions and then answering them. In the first week, they can use maps as a text feature. The second week, they reinforce this skill and review the related strategy, using the text feature of Venn diagrams to show similarities and differences. The third week, teachers focus on teaching students the skill of drawing conclusions from the text they read. They support this by teaching them the strategy of monitoring their comprehension by using the text feature of symbolism in writing. The fourth week, teachers reinforce the skill of drawing conclusions from reading text by reviewing the comprehension monitoring strategy.

Teachers could use an instructional sequence for fifth-grade reading comprehension containing eight units, each four weeks long. In each unit they would teach one or two skills and strategies using related text features. For example, when teachers have taught students the skill of paraphrasing text and the strategy of making predictions about text in previous units, in the eighth unit they can review these with students during its first week using the text feature of charts. The second week of this unit, teachers can review the skill of sequencing events and the strategy of making inferences they previously taught by using the text feature of the timeline for sequences. The third week, they can review the previously taught strategy of making connections and skill of drawing conclusions by using the text feature of point of view. In the fourth week of the unit, teachers can review with students the skill of generalizing about text and the strategy of visualization that they taught earlier.

In fifth grade, teachers might use an eight-unit instructional sequence of four-week units covering various skills and strategies for reading comprehension, using associated text features. For example, in the seventh of eight units, teachers can review skills and strategies they have taught the students in previous units. The first week, they can review the skill of generalization and the strategy of visualization they previously taught students by using the associated text feature of flowcharts. The second week, they can review the skill of telling fact from opinion and the strategy of determining the important information in a text that they taught earlier by using the text feature of subheadings. The third week, they can review with students the strategy of monitoring their comprehension and the skill of determining the author's purpose by using the text feature of foreshadowing. The fourth week, teachers can review with students the previously taught skill of comparison and contrast and strategy of asking and answering questions about the text.

Developing academic language

Academic language exceeds just the words of any specific academic vocabulary. To develop academic language, students need knowledge in the following areas: (1) Understanding the phonological features of English, like sound patterns, stress patterns, and intonation. (2) Lexical knowledge, including the parts of speech; word formation using roots, prefixes, and suffixes; grammatical parameters for forming and using words; and knowledge of specific academic vocabularies. (3) Grammatical competence, including understanding and accurately applying common morphological and syntactic elements and their functions. (4) Discourse, such as initiating conversations using appropriate greetings, which aids students in organized, coherent communication using the meanings and components of language. (5) Cognition, including not only associating letters with sounds and words with meanings for comprehending text, but moreover being able to make inferences, predictions, and achieve synthesis of meaning for constructing and transforming one's comprehension of what information was communicated.

To use academic language proficiently, students require familiarity with word formation, word structures, and word usage across various academic fields. For example, students need to know word forms and meanings commonly used in different disciplines like *analyze*, *describe*, or *explain*. They must also know how roots, prefixes, and suffixes are used to form words—for understanding academic content, and for understanding the reasons for activities and assignments and following their directions. For example, knowing how words like *hypothesize* and *investigate* are formed with prefixes and suffixes allows students to understand what they mean so they know what they are expected to do. In addition to this, research studies find that students should know whether academic words are nouns, verbs, or other parts of speech; and the grammatical rules about how academic words are to be used.

Academic language versus academic vocabulary

Some people use the term "academic language" interchangeably with the term "academic vocabulary." However, academic vocabulary is just one part of the larger entity of academic language. Academic language involves multiple elements, for example phonological features, lexical knowledge, grammatical competence, discourse, and cognition. Of these, lexical knowledge encompasses knowledge of academic vocabulary. Academic vocabulary consists of words that students must understand to access the concepts involved in a particular academic discipline, and to use in order to prove that they understand these concepts. Academic vocabulary is often characterized as having three tiers defining different word types. Tier 1 represents non-academic, high-frequency words used across various contexts, such as *sleep* or *flower*. Tier 2 represents academic words that are not specialized but used across various academic subjects, such as *illustrate* or *predict*. Tier 3 represents technical or specialized areas specific to certain academic disciplines and content areas, such as *organism* or *fulcrum*. Academic vocabulary skills are required and critical parts of academic language, but alone are not enough to build strong academic language with its multiple elements.

Different types of language comprising academic language

Academic language can be viewed as comprising three language types: (1) The language of instruction. This means words used in teaching and learning academic content. It can include using strategies, like reading comprehension strategies for cause-and-effect or prediction and inference; or pre-writing strategies, like the PLEASE strategy for writing paragraphs (Harris and Graham, 2005): Pick a topic, List your ideas, Evaluate the list, Activate your paragraph using a topic sentence, Supply supporting sentences, and End the paragraph with a concluding sentence. (2) The language of text. This means words related to the book/passage/unit/theme/content studied. For example, with a unit or theme on geology, the language of text might include words like *sedimentary*, *igneous*, *metamorphic*, *magma*, *lava*, *intrusive*, *extrusive*, and so on. (3) Multisyllabic words incorporating Greek and Latin roots, prefixes, and suffixes; for example, *physiology, informational,* and so on. Understanding things like word families (e.g., *depend, dependent, dependency, dependable*), word meanings and formation, and grammatical word forms and their creation can help students to develop their academic language.

Grammatical competence as a feature of academic language

Grammatical competence refers to the understanding of the rules of the English language and the ability to apply them appropriately. This application is necessary on two levels: in everyday conversational or informal English, and also in academic English. It includes being able to form simple and grammatically correct sentences, and complex sentences having subordinate/dependent clauses. For example, *We go to school every day* is a simple sentence, while *We go to school every day so we can learn* is a complex sentence. It also requires being able to apply knowledge about the noun system, which includes correctly adding plural endings like *-s*, using irregular plurals (e.g., *was/were*), using indefinite and definite articles (e.g., *a* and *the*), and demonstratives (e.g., *those*). Additionally, grammatically competent students must be able to understand the verb system and apply it correctly with regular and irregular verbs using all verb tenses—present, past, present perfect, present progressive/continuous, future, modal, habitual past with *would;* verbs plus complements (e.g., *He likes camping*); contractions; and phrasal verbs (e.g., *bump into* or *put down*).

For grammatical competence, students must not only be able to form grammatically correct sentences and use the noun and verb systems, they must also understand and apply knowledge about complex clause structures and syntactic structures and learn the grammatical features for new nouns. In academic English, sentences are often compound, complex, or compound-complex rather than simple. Compound sentences have two independent clauses connected by a coordinating conjunction (e.g., *I called her, but she did not answer*). Complex sentences have an independent clause plus one or more dependent clauses. Subordinators, such as *when*, *after*, *since*, *although*, or *because*; or relative pronouns like *who*, *which*, or *that*, are always used to connect the subordinate/dependent clause(s) to the independent clause. For example, *The students are busy studying because their teacher is giving them a test tomorrow*. Compound-complex sentences contain two independent clauses and one or more dependent clauses (e.g., *The students, who wanted good grades, studied hard, and they all passed the test*). Students must also master passive voice, ergative verbs/structures, prepositional phrases, and nominalization of newly acquired nouns.

Word families

Word families are groups of words all formed from the same root. Their various forms are made by adding prefixes or suffixes to roots to change them to different parts of speech. For example, *contribute* is a verb meaning to give, supply, or add. It is formed from the Latin prefix *com-*, meaning with or together; and the Latin word *tribuare*, meaning to grant. Adding the Latin suffix *–tion*, which denotes a state, thing, action, or associated meaning, changes the *contribu-* root/stem from verb to noun meaning something given, supplied, or added. Appending the suffix *–able* forms the adjective *contributable*, meaning able to be given, supplied, or added. Word families thus include nouns, verbs, and adjectives. Similar examples include *rely, reliable, reliant,* and *reliance*; *expend, expendable, expense,* and *expenditure*; and *perceive, perceptive,* and *perception*. Teachers should consider how each word in a family is formed from the root or base verb. They should think about how to instruct their students about word families and what academic language to use, what kinds of activities they could use to engage students in word-building for understanding the word family concept, and additional word families.

Metacognition

Metacognition is defined as "thinking about thinking," i.e., thinking about the process of thinking itself. To attain control over their reading, good readers use metacognitive strategies. For example, they may determine their reason(s) for reading and preview their texts before they read. While they are reading, they may review whether they understand the text; resolve any comprehension challenges they encounter; and vary their reading rates according to the level of difficulty of the individual text. After reading, they check their comprehension of the text. Student strategies for self-monitoring comprehension include locating a problem; e.g., a specific paragraph and page they don't understand; identifying an author's specific sentence/statement whose meaning they don't understand; rephrasing a challenging passage or sentence using their own words to clarify its meaning; reviewing parts of the text they read earlier to inform and help themselves understand parts they are currently reading; and looking ahead for more information in the text that may explain what they are currently reading.

Metacognitive strategies

Metacognitive strategies are any learning strategies that involve rising above the thought process to think about one's own cognitive processes, i.e., "thinking about thinking." Many metacognitive strategies are used with facility by good readers. Research finds the previous knowledge and internal dialogue with which readers approach reading are responsible for 50 percent of their reading comprehension. Think-Alouds are strategies employing such internal dialogues with texts and authors. When teachers model these dialogues for students using Think-Alouds, the students learn to "talk to the text," which produces significant increases in both comprehension and memory retention. Teacher modeling via Think-Alouds teaches students self-monitoring strategies. Students practicing these have superior comprehension than students not practicing them. Teachers should choose a short passage with a beginning, middle, and end. They inform students they will be experiencing the world of their own thoughts as readers, which differ from others' thoughts. Teachers should also tell students that reading involves not simply recognizing words, but making meaning from the text, and that making said meaning can attain better reading comprehension.

Instructing students in establishing effective Think-Alouds

"Talking to the text" refers to conducting an internal dialogue with the text and its author while reading. Doing this brings significant improvements in reading comprehension and retention of the content read. Students do not absorb this process incidentally; they must learn it through modeling by their teachers. Teachers can effectively model talking to the text and author by using the Think-Aloud metacognitive strategy. After selecting a short text passage and explaining to students that they will be exploring the world of their own unique thoughts, that reading entails constructing meaning from text, and that their comprehension can improve, teachers should begin reading the selected passage aloud. After a few lines, teachers externalize and model their own thoughts by changing the volume, accent, or pitch of their voice. Then they stop and explain to students the meaning of this vocal alteration. They consistently continue the alteration throughout. Teachers should voice thoughts concisely, focused on the text itself more than their personal experiences with it.

Students understand and remember text content better from conducting internal dialogues as they read, i.e., by "talking to the text" and author. Students generally do not learn this automatically, but must learn it through effective teacher modeling. When teachers model for students, they read a selected passage aloud, periodically inserting comments reflecting their thoughts. Teachers should not interrupt the flow of their reading aloud, and they should maintain awareness of the meaning in the text. They should insert their thoughts or commentary only about once every one or two paragraphs rather than commenting frequently. Also, comments should address both the text itself and the text's author. Teachers can obtain feedback on their Think-Aloud effectiveness by asking students if it helped them understand the text better than if they had simply read it without actively thinking about it. Affirmative student responses indicate the teacher's Think-Aloud effectiveness. Teachers should then have students practice in pairs to do their own Think-Alouds. Think-Alouds should be frequently repeated with both informational and narrative text genres.

Contextual clues

An important strategy to aid reading comprehension and build vocabulary is using clues in the context of the text to decipher the meanings of unfamiliar words. Teachers can instruct students in identifying such contextual clues by teaching them a useful stepwise strategy for finding categories of context clues: FP'S BAG SALE, an acronym for its steps. It stands for Finish, Pronounce, Syllables, Before, After, Grammar; Synonym, Antonym, Logic, and Example. Students should follow these steps until they get an idea of the meaning of an unfamiliar word in text. The first six steps involve trying to comprehend the word in its presented context. Finish – the sentence: examine how an unfamiliar word fits into the sentence context. Pronounce – the word aloud; hearing it can yield clues to its meaning. Syllables – examining each part of a word can hint at its meaning. Before – reading the sentence preceding the word may afford clues to its meaning. After – reading the sentence following the word can provide an example, explanation, or definition of the word. Grammar – the word's part of speech, grammatical relationship to other words, sentence position, and ending can all inform meaning.

The name of the FP'S BAG SALE reading strategy is an acronym reflecting the initials of each step in the procedure: Finish, Pronounce, Syllables, Before, After, Grammar; Synonym, Antonym, Logic, and Example. Students follow each named step to look in the context of what they are reading for clues to the meanings of words they do not know. The FP'S BAG portion involves Finishing the sentence, Pronouncing the word, examining its Syllables, reading the sentences Before and After it, and understanding the word's role in the sentence's Grammar. The SALE portion reflects categories of contextual clues: Synonym – the text may use synonyms, including appositives, to define a word. Antonym – similarly, the text may provide an opposite to define a word. Logic – students may be able to use their own knowledge of the text's structure and content to inform the meaning of an unfamiliar word. Example – if an unfamiliar word is part of a list of examples, or is itself an example, this can give clues to its meaning.

SCRIP

SCRIP is a set of five reading comprehension strategies. The letters in its title acronym stand for: Summarize, Connect, Rethink, Interpret, and Predict. Students can "Connect" with the text by observing the relationship among portions of text, which may consist of similarities or differences, sequences of events or ideas, and cause-and-effect relationships, to name a few. They can Connect by studying the relationship of a portion of text to something outside it, such as another book, a historical event, or a movie or TV show. They can additionally Connect by relating a portion of the text to their own personal life experiences. "Rethink" refers to rereading. Any time that students are confused while reading a text, or they have lost track of the author's train of thought, they should Rethink, which requires rereading the part of the text they have just read. Reviewing what they just read will enhance their understanding of it. Rereading can also enable students to understand the text differently than they did upon their first reading of it.

A group of five strategies to facilitate reading comprehension is named SCRIP. This acronym stands for Summarize, Connect, Rethink, Interpret, and Predict. The "Interpret" strategy involves focusing on what the author of a text meant by what he or she wrote. Authors sometimes state directly what they mean in their writing. Or authors may only hint or suggest their meaning, deliberately leaving it to readers to reach their own conclusions about what the author meant. When authors hint at or suggest their meaning, readers can identify such hints in the emotional and/or attitudinal tone of the writing, the author's choice of words, or in other portions that more directly indicate their meaning. The "Predict" strategy involves informed guesswork as to what the author will say next or what events will occur next in a text. Readers who make good predictions utilize clues available in the text to guess what will logically follow. Proficient readers also test their predictions against what is actually said or occurs next in the text.

Metacognitive process that affords better reading comprehension

Readers who interact effectively with text content enjoy better comprehension. Such interaction is triggered by cueing strategies. Studies show that readers who use self-questioning to monitor their reading internally understand and remember content better than those who read text passively without actively thinking about it. A set of reading comprehension strategies called SCRIP reflects its five strategies in its title acronym: Summarize, Connect, Rethink, Interpret, and Predict. Teachers should explicitly model and teach these strategies. They should focus on one strategy at a time with a text. They should demonstrate the SCRIP strategies using both narrative and informational texts. Teachers should assign students to practice writing down and saying the responses in SCRIP. They can also copy and distribute SCRIP bookmarks to students, and/or post SCRIP charts in classrooms. "Summarize," the first step of SCRIP, refers to synthesizing the main ideas and significant details of a text in abbreviated form. Summarizing at key transitional junctures in the author's thought sequence, which can necessitate reader re-skimming of those portions, is more beneficial than summarizing the entire reading.

Helping students to respond to literature and make connections with literary text

In order to develop student skills in literary response, teachers can engage them in reading literary works of high quality, and/or listening to these being read aloud. They can involve students in strategies and activities that will clarify literary text and help them to understand it. Teachers should access existing student knowledge and connect it with their responses to the literary text that they are reading. They can do this through providing activities like Readers' Theaters and literature circles, keeping reading logs, holding discussions across the curriculum, and writing essays about literary works that they have read. They can also engage their students in varied literary response activities, such as identifying the main problem in a story, creating semantic webs based on literary readings, constructing trait charts based on literary characters, analyzing various genres of literature, and writing book reports.

Levels of reading comprehension

The three levels of reading comprehension are literal comprehension, inferential comprehension, and evaluative comprehension. At the literal level, student reading comprehension skills include being able to identify the main idea in text, recognize patterns in a text, identify the sequence used in a text, identify cause and effect relationships in a text, and making these identifications with clarity and explicitness. At the inferential level, student reading comprehension skills include being able to draw inferences about things that the author has not directly stated in the text. For example, students should be able to recognize implied comparisons, make predictions about text based on the portions they have already read, draw conclusions based on the text, and identify cause-and-effect relationships the author has not explicitly expressed. At the evaluative level, student reading comprehension skills include reading critically, being able to differentiate facts from opinions, detecting flawed reasoning and propaganda, and identifying unsupported inferences in text.

Skills versus strategies in reading comprehension

Some experts characterize skills and strategies for reading comprehension as respective stages of development in learning. They perceive a skill as something that a student is learning or has learned, and a strategy as a skill that a student has not only learned but can also apply independently. When teachers instruct students in the literal, inferential, and evaluative levels of reading comprehension, they should include direct and explicit instruction in reading comprehension skills. Teachers should model the comprehension skills associated with each of these three levels. They should give students guided practice in applying reading comprehension skills. When students gain sufficient experience, teachers should also provide them with opportunities for independent practice of these skills. Teachers should identify and select instructional materials and resources that will support their effective instruction of students, and the students' effective practice, in the three levels of reading comprehension.

Student reading comprehension of literary and narrative text

Teachers should instruct students that their comprehension of the text they read must be both active and purposeful. Teachers should also practice and model these principles. When teachers provide students with instructional activities to build their vocabularies—both directly and indirectly—and develop their reading fluency, they are also building their reading comprehension skills. Teachers should not only instruct students in strategies to facilitate reading comprehension, they should also show students how to apply these strategies throughout their reading. Such strategies include activating their existing knowledge, recognizing story structures in narrative text, retelling and summarizing narrative content, generating and answering questions about the text, using visualization, comparing and contrasting elements of the text, previewing text, making predictions, using semantic and graphic organizers, and monitoring their own reading comprehension. In addition to direct instruction for reading comprehension, teachers should model reading strategies for students and provide them with guided practice and opportunities to apply comprehension skills independently. Teachers should also give students activities promoting connections between reading and writing.

Comprehension skills needed for reading expository and informational texts

Expository and informational texts use various organizational patterns like cause-and-effect, problem and solution, comparison and contrast, and more. This variety makes expository and informational texts more challenging for students to comprehend than traditional narrative and story texts. However, research finds that children in the elementary grades can indeed learn to differentiate narrative versus expository/informational text and, given proper instruction, understand the structural features of expository and informational texts. Using a chosen framework consistently, such as K-W-L questions (What do you Know? What do you Want to know? What did you Learn?) or questions specific to certain text content, like books about famous people or animals, gives students a predictable structure for gaining comprehension of expository or informational text. For books about animals, for example, teachers can ask students: What kind of animals are these? What do they look like? Where do they live? How do they survive? What do they eat? What threatens their survival? What challenges do they have? And what is interesting and/or unusual about them?

For reading expository texts with comprehension, teachers can use explicit oral language activities like introducing and explaining the key vocabulary words in text before students read it, orally previewing the content of text before reading and orally reviewing the content after reading, and engaging students in orally summarizing and paraphrasing the text they read. Teachers can also use explicit writing activities, such as having students write summaries of text, paraphrasing text in their own written words, and developing graphic organizers to show the structure and content of text visually. They should instruct students explicitly in taking notes, making outlines, and other study skills; and in techniques for the location, retrieval, and retention of information in reference materials as well as expository texts. Teachers should also explicitly instruct students in asking questions, evaluating questions, identifying research topics, conducting research, and managing information through the application of technology to develop their research skills. Teachers' instruction in these skills of comprehension, study and research should meet the needs of all learners in their classrooms.

Research findings about elementary-age students' comprehension of expository texts versus narrative texts

Researchers and educators are both concerned about the respective significance of expository and narrative text in elementary reading curricula. Studies show strongly that children demonstrate better reading comprehension of narrative than expository texts. In fact, this is not only in the United States but in multiple nations (35 countries, NCES, 2001), where no students scored significantly higher with expository comprehension. Educational implications of this difference include that secondary and post-secondary education involve much more expository than narrative text overall, so elementary students may be inadequately prepared. Also, different narrative versus expository items and definitions of each in assessments pose problems with interpreting results. Moreover, remediation is difficult until educators know the reason (or reasons) for these differences. Some researchers believe students support comprehension using their preconceived ideas and expectations regarding text; this offers hope in that exposure could determine and thus change the disparity. Elementary literacy instruction currently favors narrative over expository text. But if disparate schemata are needed to comprehend expository versus narrative texts, then equal proficiency in each requires equal exposure.

Expository text materials and expository text structures that students need to understand

Expository or informational text materials include such forms as websites, user manuals, research reports, news articles, and textbooks. Teachers need to apply explicit instructional strategies to further student comprehension of such expository text at the level of the word, the sentence, the paragraph, and the whole text. They need to assist students in expository text comprehension by helping them to understand the text structures commonly utilized, like cause-and-effect, comparison and contrast, chronological sequence, and problem and solution. Teachers also need to instruct students in recognizing and addressing text features related to these various text structures, such as topic sentences, transitional sentences, and

- 46 -

concluding sentences. They also need to instruct students explicitly to help them identify various text features that support their comprehending expository texts. These include explanatory features like tables of contents, glossaries, and indexes; typographical features like color-coded text, underlining, italicized and bold-faced text; and graphical features like illustrations, diagrams, maps, and charts.

Characteristics of narrative versus expository text and the respective schemata (mental constructs) they require students to apply for comprehension

Traditional narratives depict relationships among settings, plots, and characters. They feature concluding global endings and clearly delineate elements like beginnings and endings and settings and goal accomplishment. Sociolinguistic models of narrative identify these narrative elements: abstract, orientation, complication, evaluation, result, and coda. Studies find the cognitive processes of organization, information reduction, storage, and retrieval affected by narrative structure. Expository structure primarily employs logic, reason, and declarative statements. It is evaluated by its strength of argumentation and accuracy. It is organized into declarations whereby readers can follow the flow of text via causality and logic. Analysis of exposition typically refers to propositional structure. Authors begin with a main proposition, which organizes later propositions and connects these to the author's primary goals. One caveat with knowing such contrasts and the corresponding schemata they require is that this does not reveal their effects on comprehension, which then limits both research and practical application. To inform instruction, researchers also study the respective scopes of processing readers use for narrative versus expository text.

Scope of processing relative to reading comprehension

Processing scope is defined along a continuum of local to global. Local processing is at the phrase and sentence level. For example, when reading the sentence, "She ran to the bank to save the child from drowning," the reader cannot determine which meaning of the word "bank" is used—a riverbank—until the sentence's last word. If instead of "...drowning," the sentence ended "...being shot by armed robbers," then "bank" would have the alternative meaning of a financial building. Local processing allows coherence in local interpretation, but does not guarantee consistency across text or even across sentences. Global processing is required, for example, when reading a murder mystery: solving it necessitates tracing suspect activities and corroborating alibis throughout the narrative. Expository texts, with their extended reasoning and argumentation, also demand global processing to evaluate the compatibility of different points and/or subject factors not addressed. Researchers find readers usually apply processing scope for minimal acceptable coherence, making only automatic connections from immediately available information. Therefore, readers will not construct global processing unless circumstances demand it.

Scopes of reader processing for expository versus narrative text, differential effects of reading interventions with each text genre, and their resulting influences on texts used

Depending on which schemata the texts that students read are based upon, they could influence the readers to use different processing scopes. Narrative texts are processed more globally, dictating a broader scope of processing. Some researchers even believe that the instructional technique of story mapping is still insufficient to encompass global reader responses that connect reading comprehension of narratives to the readers' personal experiences. Expository texts are processed more locally, for their discrete propositions versus their overall structure. Interventions to enhance processing and integration levels are found more effective for reading exposition than narrative. This finding suggests that students process exposition less globally without explicit prompting. Such interventions may focus on local processing of antecedent-consequence relationships, establishment of certain claims before making others, and/or rhetorical robustness. The results are texts following either local models or idiosyncratic, uneven global models for comprehension. Some researchers attribute the disparity in greater student comprehension of narrative than exposition in part to greater structural similarity among narrative texts than among expository texts.

Challenges for educational researchers to separate and compare the features of narrative text and expository text

In comparing the text genres of narrative and exposition, structural differences and semantic differences have frequently been confounded. It is difficult for researchers to isolate the features of each text genre. Exposition often becomes equated with academic textbooks, and narrative with fiction. This can lead to conflation of the concept of exposition with textbooks and the concept of narrative with fiction. Such assumptions are limited, however, because subject areas like history commonly use informational narratives, possibly even more often than not. Moreover, some text materials such as biographies, autobiographies, and newspaper articles combine elements of both narrative and exposition within the same text. In these cases it is hard to ascertain the amount of each genre's contribution to the whole. Also, measures assessing student results vary greatly among research studies, making it hard to determine whether genre or task requirements cause differences. Some researchers find comparing student performance using within-subjects design, equivalent texts, and tasks separating local from global processing help to remove many confounding variables.

Comparing student reading comprehension of narrative versus expository texts using different tasks that require participants to use either global or local processing

It is often difficult for educational researchers to separate the features of narrative and expository text genres. This is due to multiple factors, such as the association of each genre with limited examples of each—such as narrative with fiction and exposition with academic textbooks—that some text types combine elements of both narrative and exposition. Another cause is that different research studies use disparate tasks to assess student results, confounding text genre with task requirements as causing student outcomes. Some researchers believe using equivalent texts, designing tasks requiring either local or global processing, and using within-subjects design to compare student performance can eliminate most confounding variables. They reason that if students can more easily construct schemata for text with narrative structure, then tasks demanding global processing should yield better performance with narrative, and that tasks needing only local processing should yield similar results with both narrative and exposition. Educational implications are that results would help predict which assessments and items would yield narrative-expository differences and guide designing activities supporting reading skills development with both genres.

Research findings about student preferences, motivation, interest, and comprehension related to reading narrative versus expository texts

Some researchers who compared student comprehension and recall of narrative versus expository text found no differences in performance between genres when students needed only local processing, as when answering questions during reading, asked one page at a time. However, students performed better with narrative when global processing was required, as when retelling an entire text passage after reading. These and previous researchers found students have no preference for either genre and enjoy both. They conclude student difficulties with exposition are not from lack of interest, comprehension, or motivation and/or engagement, but because its structure is less obvious, familiar, and utile than narrative structure. They recommend that formal and informal assessments of student performance across genres be viewed separately from text characteristics such as imagery and fictional attributes, and also from motivational factors such as expectancy and interest. Also, while instruction in underlying text structure has traditionally focused mainly on narrative, teachers should also give explicit instruction of exposition. This is especially necessary if students have trouble recognizing and using expository structure to recall material.

Reading Assessment and Instruction

Creating effective literacy learning environments

Young children need print-rich learning environments that facilitate and enhance their phonological awareness and supply them with ongoing reinforcement of direct instruction. Teachers should provide young children with continual, ready access to books and other literary materials, rather than simply storing them on shelves. They should expose young children to many varieties of print. A classroom library containing both fiction and non-fiction books should be located centrally, and include newspapers, magazines, telephone books, restaurant menus, etc. Teachers should also integrate literacy across the curriculum by reading and assigning texts that support their learning units in subjects such as mathematics, sciences, and social studies. For example, they can teach sequencing during science experiments by using graphic organizers. They can visually display the relevant number words and math terms during classroom calculations so the children can see these math processes represented phonetically as they work with them

Stimulating literacy development

In addition to providing continual, easy exposure and access to reading and writing materials, continually reinforcing their direct instruction, and integrating literacy across the subject content curriculum, teachers should also choose literacy materials according to children's abilities and needs. They should include texts for various reading levels in their classroom libraries to allow all children to experience reading success. They can supply concrete objects, such as picture cards of alphabet letters and plastic letter manipulatives, which help beginning readers to decode printed words. They can borrow more sophisticated books from teachers of higher grades to provide challenges for more advanced young readers. Teachers' daily reading aloud to classes affords their participation and motivation. Teachers can model expression by varying their voices to represent various characters in fables and fairy tales. Informal 30-minute reading periods twice weekly, in which children and teachers all read silently for pleasure, also enhance motivation. Technology can support literacy development; for example, teachers and students can use digital dry-erase whiteboards for instruction in phonics, vocabulary, and text structure.

Assessment and instructional planning relative to reading and writing

Young children should undergo initial screening to determine their literacy levels before teachers plan their instruction. Children's literacy status and progress should also be assessed frequently and continuously, both to monitor their learning and to inform instructional planning. Long-term research into student reading development shows that the majority of third-graders evidencing weak reading skills, also had difficulty with phonological awareness and phonologically related reading skills from the time they first began school. Moreover, assessment identifies students' specific areas of weakness with the highest probabilities of causing difficulties with reading. This enables teachers to design instructional plans that target these specific weaknesses and their remediation. This targeted instruction frequently averts students' failing at reading later on in school, as well as promoting most students' reading development.

Reading instruction

One part of effective reading instruction involves (1) phonemic awareness, (2) knowledge of letters, and (3) print concepts. Variations in young children's early success with reading and spelling are not due as much to their intelligence, levels of maturity, or listening comprehension, as to their levels of phonemic awareness and knowledge of letter-sound correspondences. Children who are found to have poor development of phonemic awareness by the end of kindergarten are more likely to read poorly in later grades. Teachers can mitigate young children's risk of later failure in reading by giving them explicit instruction in identifying sounds, matching phonemes, segmenting words into phonemes, and blending phonemes into words, and associating sounds and their symbols. This type of explicit instruction also speeds up the early acquisition of reading and spelling for all young children.

Critical thinking

When children read, their ability to think deeply about the book or its subject is a simple example of critical thinking, which takes time, experiences, and conversations to develop, and which they will need throughout life. As important as it is for adults to read to and with the youngest children, adults should also continue reading with children who can read independently. This helps children handle more challenging books with more complicated plots, more difficult vocabulary, and longer chapters and total length. Adults model and instruct patience and persistence and supply information, guidance, and support for children by working through challenging books together. To think critically, readers must slow down; adults must take time to help children reflect upon what they read. They might discuss what we learn about a character's personality from his/her actions; or the importance to the overall message of a book's setting; or a conflict in the plot. Adults can ask more open-ended questions, for which children can give many correct answers.

One instructional technique to help students apply critical thinking to reading content-area texts is the I-Chart Procedure (Hoffman, 1997). It has three stages: Planning, Interacting, and Integrating and Evaluating. Planning: students identify a topic to study from their subject-area texts. They develop questions to answer in reading. They then make a big chart for recording information they will collect, including entries of teacher and student questions; sources; the topic; what they know; other interesting information, e.g., figures and/or facts; and other questions. Gathering topic-related materials completes this stage. Interacting: students record their existing topic knowledge, plus other information they may collect. The teacher also elicits and records pertinent student questions. With teacher guidance, students read and discuss information sources. Integrating and Evaluating: students summarize each charted question, including collected information; compare summaries to background knowledge; clarify as needed; discuss what they learned; additionally research unanswered questions; and report their findings to the class. Teachers initially provide scaffolding—modeling and directing—and gradually withdraw support as students independently apply strategies

K-W-L instructional procedure

K-W-L (Ogle, 1986) stands for Know, Want, and Learned—i.e., What I Know, What I Want to Learn, and What I Learned. These are the areas covered by each step of this procedure, which helps students learn thinking habits related to good reading—specifically, determining their purposes for reading a text, and activating their background knowledge when reading new material. In the Know step, students discuss what they already know about a topic in the text they will read. Teachers have students list topic-related concepts, and then organize their thoughts into general categories. Thus, students relate new information they read to their existing knowledge. In the Want step, students learn to establish their own purposes for reading, and in this way, also actively self-monitor their comprehension. In the Learned step, students' expressing information in their own terms improves their realizing what they do and do not know. Following these steps reinforces students' learning from reading, engages them in good reading habits, and teaches them metacognition about their own processes of reading.

Questioning the Author

Questioning the Author (Beck et al, 1997) is a procedure that stimulates students to reflect on what an author is trying to say in expository text that they read. This reflection is intended to help students create mental representations of the information they read. Teachers collaborate with students to understand the text, clarify any confusing parts, and improve comprehension. The procedure incorporates discussion, instruction in reading comprehension strategies, and self-explanation by the students. To help students realize that some parts of texts can be confusing and limit their comprehension, the teacher models questioning techniques. The class will focus on a certain portion of a text, and the teacher will ask questions, such as, "What is the author trying to say?" "Why does the author say this?" "What did the author mean by this?" etc. The teacher and students discuss what strategies they can resort to when they encounter comprehension difficulties. Students learn to tackle challenging text by imitating the teacher's questioning models.

Decoding

Basically, being able to apply one's knowledge of patterns in printed letters and of correspondences between letters and the sounds they represent, and to pronounce printed words correctly, constitute word decoding. When children understand letter patterns and letter-sound relationships, this affords them the capacity for quick recognition of familiar words, and for deciphering unfamiliar words. While children have been observed to arrive at a comprehension of some relationships of letters and sounds by themselves, the majority of children will become more successful at understanding these when they are also given explicit instruction in decoding. One way that educators can give such explicit teaching is through instruction in phonics. Phonics teaches children the principles that guide the relationships of letters to sounds; it teaches them the process of sounding out printed words they see; and it teaches them the exceptions to the rules that are the main guiding principles of the relationships of letters and sounds.

Signs that parents may observe that can indicate difficulties with phonics and decoding

Parents observing their children trying to read at home may notice several areas of difficulty with phonics and decoding. For example, a parent may find s/he often tells the child what many printed words say because the child cannot decipher them and gets "stuck." Parents may observe their child reading at a very slow rate because s/he takes so much time figuring out many of the words. The parents may find their child is so preoccupied with attempting to sound out words that s/he demonstrates little comprehension of the reading. Parents may realize their child does not seem to know how to read words by synthesizing the information in the reading. They may find if they try to guide their child by telling them to "sound out" words, the child's frustration only increases. In addition, parents may notice their child uses only the first one or two letters of a word to guess at it, rather than focusing on all printed letters.

Factors teachers may observe that can indicate a student might have difficulty with phonics and decoding

Teachers may notice that a student who makes numerous spelling errors and has trouble reading also finds it difficult to match letters with the sounds they represent. Difficulty with phonics and letter-sound correspondences usually impedes reading and spelling. A teacher may observe that a student's decoding of words is very laborious. A student who finds it hard to spell or read phonetically likely has decoding and phonics deficits. When the teacher designs activities using phonics and phonetic patterns, students who have marked trouble with these are apt to have problems with decoding words and using phonics. Students who tend to hazard guesses at printed words, based only on the first letter or couple of letters, are more likely to have decoding deficiencies, so they avoid sounding out words. A teacher may find that even after s/he has taught several letter sounds or patterns, the student cannot identify these in reading, and/or the student's writing samples do not reflect these.

Word-decoding and phonics strategies and activities

When parents and teachers find that some children have difficulty with phonics principles and decoding printed words, they can give them some strategies to help themselves. For example, adults can give children magnetized letters to play with, and ask them to sing the Alphabet Song while arranging the letters into alphabetical order as rapidly as they can. Adults can guide children to observe the print and writing in materials inside the household and on signs outdoors to see whether they can find letter patterns and words that they recognize. Parents and teachers can advise children to compose text messages, e-mails, written/typed notes and letters to their relatives and friends. Adults can also remind children as they write these communications to attend to each speech sound they are hearing as they write them down. Adults should also remind children to attend closely to every letter in a printed word to try to sound it out, rather than only the first one or two letters.

With young children beginning to read, parents can help them learn the alphabet letters and their corresponding speech sounds. Periodically, parents should point to letters and have children name them. Parents can help children form associations between words they see on signs and/or in newspapers, etc., and the school lessons on sounds and letters they are learning. Parents can encourage and reinforce children's using their knowledge of sounds and letters to write notes, letters, e-mails, etc. When children encounter words with irregular spellings (e.g. was, said, or are), parents should discuss these with them regularly so they learn to recognize them on sight, since they do not fit normal letter-sound rules. Parents can take advantage of computer software for developing phonics and early literacy skills, including some programs featuring writing support. For example, some software programs give children practice with short vs. long vowel sounds, and with constructing compound words; others invite children to construct sentences, which are then acted out by animated characters.

To help young children in developing early literacy skills, when teaching a specific phoneme (speech sound), teachers can give children three-dimensional objects and pictures, and have them sort these by that sound. Teachers should repeatedly have children say the letter's sound aloud every time they identify or differentiate it. To establish a solid foundation for reading and writing, teachers should use explicit and systematic instruction in phonics. If the school's curriculum materials are not designed for systematic, explicit phonics instruction, teachers should consult their reading specialists or school principals. Experts deem it best to begin this early phonics instruction by first grade. To help them comprehend the function of phonics, teachers should not only teach students phonics information, but also have students apply this learning by engaging them in reading and writing activities that demand such application. Concrete manipulatives, such as magnetized letters, counters, sound boxes, etc., help younger students learn letter-sound correspondences. Teachers can also group students based on their literacy needs, delivering more instruction where indicated.

Identifying books according to their levels of age-appropriateness

Some systems used to classify reading materials for the age and grade levels they best apply to are the Basal Level or PALS (Phonological Awareness Literacy Screening) system; the Guided Reading system; the Reading Recovery system; the Developmental Reading Assessment (DRA) level system; and the Rigby PM system. Books for typical kindergarten students are classified at the Readiness level by the PALS/Basal Level system; at Level A in the Guided Reading system; and at Level 1 in Reading Recovery, DRA, and Benchmark 1 in the Rigby PM system. In grades K and/or 1, students are normally at the Continued Readiness level in Basal Level/PALS; level B in Guided Reading; and at Level 2 in the Reading Recovery and DRA systems and Benchmark 2 in the Rigby PM system. Also in grades K/1, reading at the PP1(A) [Preschool-Primary] level in Basal Level/PALS is level C in Guided Reading; 3 and 4 in Reading Recovery; 3 in DRA; and Benchmarks 3 and 4 in Rigby PM.

Categorizing books by their reading grade levels

Leveling systems that help educators and parents choose texts appropriate for various reading levels include the PALS (Phonological Awareness Literacy Screening)/Basal Level system; the Guided Reading system; the Reading Recovery system; the DRA (Developmental Reading Assessment) system; the Rigby PM system of benchmarks; and the Lexile Framework. For typical 1st/2nd-grade readers, the PALS level is 1.2, which corresponds to Level H in Guided Reading; Levels 13 and 14 in Reading Recovery; Level 14 in DRA; Benchmark 15 in Rigby PM; and Levels 200L-400L in the Lexile Framework. 1st- and 2nd-graders at the level deemed 1.2 continued in PALS are at Level I in Guided Reading; Levels 15, 16, and 17 in Reading Recovery; Level 16 in DRA; Benchmark 16 in Rigby PM; and Levels 200L-400L in the Lexile Framework. Second-graders at Level 2.1 in PALS are at Level J in Guided Reading; Levels 18, 19, and 20 in Reading Recovery; Level 18 in DRA; Benchmark 17 in Rigby PM; and Levels 300L-500L in the Lexile Framework.

Classifying books according to the grade levels for which they are most appropriate

A number of systems have been developed assigning reading levels to books. These include the Phonological Awareness Literacy Screening (PALS)/Basal Level system; the Guided

Reading system; the Developmental Reading Assessment (DRA) system; the Rigby PM system; and the Lexile Framework. For second grade, the reading level designated "2.1 continued" by PALS corresponds to Level K in Guided Reading's classification; Level 20 in DRA; Benchmark 18 in Rigby; and Levels 300L-500L in Lexile Framework. The level designated Second/2.2 by PALS corresponds to typical 2nd- and 3rd-grade readers; levels L and M in Guided Reading; Levels 24 and 28 in DRA; Benchmarks 21 and 22 in Rigby PM; and 300L-500L in Lexile Framework. For grades 3-4, PALS uses Third; Guided Reading, Levels N, O, and P; DRA, Levels 30, 34, and 38; Rigby PM, Benchmarks 23, 24, and 25; Lexile Framework, 500L-700L. In fourth grade—Fourth in PALS—Guided Reading uses Levels Q, R, and S; DRA does not apply; Rigby PM assigns Benchmarks 26, 27, and 28, and Lexical Framework 650L-850L.

Common Core State Standards (CCSS)

The developers of the CCSS advise that while narrative is important, students must also develop skills for writing argument and persuasion that they support through text-based information. This information includes not only facts and events, but also ideas and arguments that students encounter in the texts they read. To write from textual sources, students must be able to generate their own informational text. They must learn to use evidence from texts to back up their arguments, to organize their writing to persuade the reader, and to compare multiple sources. To teach them these skills, teachers must spend less time on having students write personal narratives, and give students opportunities for writing using multiple research sources. They should give students opportunities to analyze/break down and synthesize/put together ideas they encounter. They must help students develop their own voices for arguing points using evidence. They should offer students permission to arrive at their own conclusions about what they read and articulate these conclusions.

Informational genre of books

Elementary school teachers are realizing that informational texts are important for developing children's reading and writing skills. Research finds that elementary students' knowledge of both content and genre is supported by experience with informational books, and that they use elements of this genre in their own writing from early ages. Research also implies that teachers' reading information books aloud and explicitly teaching genre elements to young students improves their instruction. Moreover, instructing students to "think like writers" as they read builds their knowledge about authors' organizational decision-making processes. Some teachers realized their students had read information texts, discussed them, written short book reports, and constructed projects about them, but never written their own information books. They assigned this, preparing students with focused read-aloud sessions explicitly analyzing the genre elements and features in the text, and systematically teaching them how to apply these in their own writing. They found this effective in helping students learn to read and write in diverse forms and for multiple audience—skills needed to communicate effectively.

Benefits of teaching expository book structures

The majority of preschool and primary school teachers are familiar with the story elements found in storybooks and other narrative texts. Many young children are also familiar with stories when they begin school, and most younger students quickly learn to identify and remember such story structures. Similarly to narrative texts, informational texts also use certain structures that teachers can teach young students to recognize. Teachers can use such expository structures to improve younger students' comprehension, which researchers have found will further benefit their understanding of content-area texts written at intermediate and higher levels. Studies have concluded that the role of the teacher is crucial in order for students to interact effectively with informational texts in the classroom. Teachers must both possess strong knowledge about informational texts, and provide their students with greater access to such books. Teachers can consult online references prepared by experts to help them make selections that have high quality and appeal highly to younger readers' interests.

Cover of a quality informational children's book

The cover of a book, being the first thing children see, should capture their attention and invite them to look inside. Experts find that illustrations or photographs that are clear and colorful, and that use bright, primary colors, are most attractive to younger children. In addition to the colors and illustrations, the book's title should grab a child's attention and should stimulate interest and inquiry in young readers. Titles should be brief enough to engage them, using words they can understand and fonts large enough for them to read easily. For example, some quality informational books which feature covers that catch children's eyes and grab their attention include Big Bugs (Simon, 2005); Fishy Tales (Lock, 2003); and Bats (Wood, 2000). Publishers of children's books such as Dorling Kindersley and National Geographic have recently issued books with covers and titles that entice children's attention and interest, setting an excellent example for the many other publishers of children's literature.

Factors regarding the content and/or topics of informational children's books that will appeal to young readers

Non-fiction books need not be dull. Young children tend to be naturally interested in many topics covered in children's literature, and their inquisitive nature attracts them to information to answer their myriad questions about life and the world. However, there are still aspects of these books that will make them even more interesting to children. Parents and teachers should look for topics in books that their children find exciting, and which include a bit of mystery as well. Authors who share fascinating factual information in the manner of tour guides will invite children to follow them into the "jungle" of information. Because our current times are considered the "information age," it is important to give children reliable and accurate content. Adults should look for authors' documentation of references, sources, and/or consultations with experts in the areas covered by their books. One example of an author highly regarded by educational experts is Seymour Simon, who has written over 200 high-quality books about diverse topics like storms, earthquakes, sharks, trucks, etc.

Adopting computer technology in schools

While educators may think classroom computers are new educational innovations, these have actually been present for over 20 years. The first recorded instance of 1:1 laptops was in 1990. In the late 1990s, Microsoft's Anytime Anywhere Learning Program initiative introduced laptops to a thousand schools. Over half of American schools had some laptops by 2005. Since their introduction, researchers have found laptops and Internet connections supply scaffolding to students for many classroom topics, building students' background knowledge. Researchers also observed greater student engagement in wireless classes, which included analysis of reading, more varied writing activities, and using software to produce media. Moreover, research has found that students attained control over reading, both on computer screens and book pages. Students in wireless classrooms discover technology has more to offer them than texting and gaming, like knowing how navigate, search for and locate information, and interpreting visual and textual elements in documents. Because today's kids see technology simply as life, education connected to their lives by technology is more engaging and motivating.

Using technology

Much instructional software exists today. For example, KidBiz Achieve 3000 is a web-based individualized reading and writing instructional program. Students each receive KidBiz e-mails with questions designed to activate their background knowledge prior to reading current events articles. Multiple articles on the same topics are provided at different reading levels: all students in a class read similar articles, but each at his/her own reading level. After replying to answer the e-mailed question, students read the article. This software also helps teachers prepare students for high-stakes, standardized, criterion-referenced tests (CRTs). The KidBiz website provides "thought questions" that supply writing prompts related to its provided articles and require students to write constructed-response questions based on what they read, similar to CRT questions. Teachers assign small-group/whole-class discussions following these activities. Students find lists of all stories their class is reading that year on a webpage, which links to a website such as Flashcard Exchange, where teachers have entered vocabulary words for each story. Students can study/practice the words for any story they select.

In a class using technology, a teacher gives an elementary school class (4th-graders, for example) an open-ended question—e.g., about an imaginary friend—and have students IM their assigned "buddy" describing him/her/it. The teacher leads class discussion about the writing trait Ideas and Content; then has them listen for examples of this as s/he reads them a picture book about an imaginary friend. The teacher has students visit a website such as www.writingfix.com, which offers interactive writing prompts guiding students to describe the imaginary friend's specific characteristics. This prepares students for a "Quick Write" (first draft). As they write, the teacher discusses individual writing and improvements with some students. Students' Quick Writes are electronically saved for revisiting and advancing through further drafts. Students use built-in software features like spell-check, grammar-check, and thesaurus for editing, learning mindfulness when they find software is not always right. Peer review is also facilitated electronically. Students print and post finished writing on the bulletin board. Such activities show smooth transitions from traditional to new literacies.

Closed-captioned and subtitled TV and movies in educational applications

Closed-captioning originally was designed to facilitate TV and movie viewing by deaf and hard-of-hearing persons. However, once this technology was available widely, it became popular with many hearing users, and has been found educationally valuable for diverse students. Federal law has mandated built-in closed-captioning on every TV set since 1993; today, movies, sports events, live news broadcasts, most TV programs, and also many online videos include closed-captions. Research studies find that students with learning disabilities

(LD), those with other academic difficulties, and those learning English as a non-native language can all benefit from classroom videos that include captions. Captioned/subtitled media can support teachers in providing differentiated instruction in classrooms. Beginning readers, struggling readers, and LD students can realize improvements in word recognition, vocabulary knowledge and acquisition, decoding skills, reading comprehension, silent reading speed, and oral reading speed. Studies find viewing video improves comprehension skills, and watching captioned video enhances vocabulary learning. Even beginning readers can benefit from captioned videos with simpler vocabularies.

Teaching young students new vocabulary words

Common instructional strategies teachers use to help young students learn new vocabulary words include: (1) Questioning – when reading aloud, teachers stop at unfamiliar words, asking students their meanings. They may also (2) supply definitions and typical applications, asking students for corresponding words, most often in embedded instruction. To elicit targeted words and reinforce word learning, teachers often (3) provide synonyms. Another strategy to clarify and expand word knowledge is (4) giving students and/or eliciting from them examples of target words. This offers opportunities to use target words; and helps students learn relationships to other words and concepts, and connect words to instances of their use. Teachers also (5) correct and/or clarify student responses, completing partial understandings and/or addressing misunderstandings to guide vocabulary knowledge; (6) extend students' word definitions, supplementing their information; (7) labeling picture-book illustrations with corresponding new words; (8) using facial, gestural, and/or auditory imagery to illustrate word meanings during read-alouds; and (9) teaching morphemic analyses of complex new words for roots and other components to figure out meanings.

Skill areas that are necessary for children to develop literacy

According to studies by the National Reading Panel, for children to develop literacy, they must have developed skills in phonemic awareness, phonics, vocabulary, comprehension, and fluency. A prerequisite to developing these five skill areas is having an understanding of how literacy works, what it does, and how it is used. While young children exposed to spoken and printed language interactions from birth often develop this understanding of the functions and applications of literacy in a natural way, children with language and learning disabilities may not. A literacy-rich environment is defined as one that provides students having disabilities with stimulation to take part in activities involving language and literacy during their everyday life routines. Stimulating such participation in and integration of language and literacy into daily living is an effective way to help disabled students begin to develop understanding of how spoken and printed language function and are used. Teaching strategies to establish literacy-rich environments can not only remediate language and literacy deficits, but also benefit all elementary-level students.

Characteristics of a literacy-rich environment in an elementary school classroom

An elementary classroom constituting a literacy-rich setting would engage all students in various literacy activities, some working individually and others in groups. Students would explore different genres of books, not only during reading periods or in the library, but during math, social studies, and science periods or lessons. The teacher might read aloud to students from a book about math during math period, and lead class discussions of the book's content, and have students explore eyewitness science books during science time to learn about scientific concepts. These activities help students experience literacy across all curriculum subject content areas. Students also use books on tapes and CD-ROMs. The classroom includes adapted materials to motivate disabled students to read and help them interact with text. Students write in notebooks and journals, write reports in all subjects, and compose books. A literacy-rich classroom environment features information resources for students including dictionaries, encyclopedias, books in varied genres, word walls, and computers, as well as teachers and peers.

Classroom materials that support literacy across the curriculum

In a classroom that supports literacy, the teacher should provide labels combining words and pictures on all objects. This continually stimulates students to associate written language with the objects and concepts it represents. Especially to support disabled students, teachers should use their particular interests and needs as a guide for labeling things. Printed directions, signs, calendars, and schedules are materials that students should use regularly in the classroom. These help students realize how language is used in everyday life. When the class is studying a certain topic, theme, or book, the teacher and students can work together to redesign the classroom using printed/written materials that reflect that topic, theme, or book. This enables students to experience fully and "live" the lesson rather than just observing it. All of the materials must be adapted for any students' special needs. For instance, in a class including blind/visually impaired students, labels, signs and other print materials can incorporate Braille words and textured surfaces.

Considerations for addressing diverse student abilities and needs

Teachers must consider the diversity among the skills and needs of their students as they design their classroom learning environments. The teachers should individualize the setting and their instruction so that these represent every student. Individualization and instructional differentiation should not only address disabled students' needs; they should also regularly provide suitable opportunities for these students to participate on an ongoing basis in activities that involve literacy and integrate it into all content areas. According to research, a salient need of students with diverse literacy backgrounds is that they often have trouble connecting new information to their existing knowledge. This ability is a critical component of learning. When teachers plan and organize their classrooms to offer literacy activities that are accessible to disabled students—and that immerse them in literacy experiences and give them opportunities to connect both new with old information, and spoken with printed language—these students can then access the general education curriculum.

Whole-class and traditional small-group classroom arrangements for reading

A major disadvantage of whole-class reading is that students who read above the average class level go unchallenged and can become bored, while students reading below average level are lost. Yet the small-group method intended to remedy this also has the drawback that, as traditionally implemented, most time is used for skill instruction, leaving far too little time for students actually to read the text. One solution is a flexible grouping model, e.g., Grouping Without Tracking (Paratore, 1990). This model uses a "sandwich" structure: teachers give students shared-reading processes at the beginning and end of the lesson, but provide differentiated instruction to two groups in the middle as they read the text.

Teachers give indirect guidance to students who can read more independently, and more direct support to struggling readers. Teachers reunite the groups to lead them in a final discussion. Students with reading difficulties gain reading proficiency and comprehension from direct teacher support, enabling them to contribute better to the whole-class discussion, so all share this experience equally.

Alternative reading and writing forms that teachers can include to help students attain greater progress in reading

When students read and write outside of school, they choose many alternative forms of reading and writing. To engage these students while they are in school, teachers should think about adding such alternative materials to their own instructional programs. For example, teachers might incorporate such media as graphic novels, magazines, newspapers, plays, anthologies of poetry, e-books and other digital/online content, and text that students have written themselves. Educational experts advise that just because it can be harder to determine the reading levels of such alternative text formats, teachers should not shy away from using them. Because they represent examples of text that people (including students) read in real life, they provide not only excellent practice for students' present and future reading of real-world materials, but also motivation to read and meaningful experiences in reading. Another boon of using these authentic, alternative texts is that they frequently incorporate multiple reading levels, so that nearly every student can read some portions of them.

Nature and prevalence of reading difficulties in school children

Young students' difficulties with reading are not characterized as existent vs. nonexistent, but rather along a continuum. This means that a broad range of students experience some kinds of reading problems. Some students have diagnoses of learning disabilities (LD) that interfere with reading easily. Even larger numbers of others are not diagnosed with LD, but nevertheless need instructional help targeting the specific problems they encounter with reading. Some experts estimate that approximately ten million children experience trouble with learning to read. However, they also find that of children with reading impairments, approximately 90-95% can surmount these problems if they are given suitable intervention at young ages. Adults should not rely on formal diagnoses as signs of reading problems; they must watch for children's progress and/or problems. Adults must first (1) ascertain accurately the type and cause of a child's reading problem; (2) give instruction targeting problem remediation and skills improvement; and (3) make accommodations for student needs and build on student strengths.

Things for adults to look for in young children that could indicate reading problems

Parents, caregivers, and teachers should attend to how each individual child is progressing in skills areas prerequisite and related to reading. For example, with preschool-aged children, adults should observe whether a child has comparatively more difficulty than his/her age peers with pronouncing words, learning the alphabet, recognizing and producing rhymes; learning colors and/or shapes of concrete objects; learning numbers; and/or learning the days of the week. Adults can also consult many sources available online and on paper that identify common developmental milestones in language development and reading development. If a child regularly demonstrates difficulty with several developmental milestones, the adult(s) should consider having the child evaluated for potential reading and/or learning disabilities. Adults should keep in mind that children learn at different rates and in different ways. However, the majority of students with normal development can read grade-level materials, with comprehension and fluency, by the end of third grade. Preventing students from falling behind grade level in reading is important, because reading problems are best remediated at early ages.

Students more likely than others to develop reading problems

While any student can have reading problems for a variety of causes, some students have higher probabilities of encountering difficulty with reading. Adults need to know about these relationships, as their knowledge can inform their monitoring of students at higher risk for deficits in reading skills. Closer monitoring enables earlier detection of problems and intervention to address them. For example, children of parents who have histories of reading problems can be more likely also to present with reading problems. Children with hearing impairments have a higher likelihood of reading problems, since the normal basis for language and reading development is auditory. Children with visual impairments are also more likely to have delays and/or deficits in visually reading print. Children who have received diagnoses of specific language impairments have a greater probability of reading problems, as do students with cognitive disabilities. In addition, children without physical or cognitive deficits who were exposed less to literacy-related knowledge and/or skills during their preschool development are found more likely to develop reading difficulties.

Reading difficulties vs. reading disabilities

Some students are not formally diagnosed with any reading or learning disability, but nevertheless struggle to read. Some such children simply progress a bit slower than their age peers. Some may need more time for learning certain concepts/skills. Some might have had prior reading instruction that was inadequate. Others might need reading instruction that is more specialized than what they have received. Regardless, students with reading difficulties need informed attention from parents, schools, and teachers to improve their reading skills. Students who do have formal diagnoses of learning disabilities (LD) are entitled to receive special education services by the federal Individuals with Disabilities Education Act (IDEA). This law also mandates that every student with a disability have an Individualized Education Program (IEP) developed for him/her. Support and services related to reading can be part of the IEP goals and objectives. Research finds that reading disabilities probably exist in at least 20% of the US population; yet among school-aged students, only around 4% receive special education services for them.

Findings of research into the prevalence and identification of reading problems

Studies investigating reading difficulties find that these exist along a continuum of reading ability; therefore, the causes of poor reading and good reading are the same. Research has identified that at least 10 million of American children read poorly. Studies show that boys and girls experience reading problems at equivalent rates; however, schools identify boys with reading problems four times more than girls. This is mostly due to behavioral factors rather than differences in learning. The identification of school-aged children with reading problems has greatly increased over time: special education statistics show that before 1980, fewer than 25% of children in special education programs were identified with learning disabilities, while more than 50% were identified with LDs by 1993. Out of all children in schools identified with LDs, 80% have primarily reading problems; of this group,

90% have difficulties specifically with developing decoding skills, which are necessary for reading fluently and with comprehension.

Beliefs about reading problems vs. what studies have found

Much research has found that the earlier a child's age when intervention begins to improve reading skills, the more effective that intervention is. However, even when reading problems have been detected early in a child's life, some adults may sometimes assume that over time, the child will "grow out" of these difficulties. Although even normally developing children progress at a variety of rates, numerous studies have demonstrated that among children who read poorly in third grade, almost ¾ of them are still reading poorly when they have reached ninth grade. The single most common source of reading difficulty is poor skills in decoding the relationships of letters to sounds. Some adults may also assume that students can overcome decoding deficiencies by context, through overall reading comprehension; however, reading comprehension is dependent on decoding skills, among others. The strongest predictor of inadequate reading comprehension is incorrect and slow decoding. Although poor reading has many causes, its characteristic decoding difficulties are primarily at the single-word level.

Results of instructional approaches to remediating reading development

When researchers compared instructional approaches emphasizing context, those using embedded phonics, and those explicitly teaching phonics to first- and second-grade students receiving Title 1 services for socially disadvantaged populations, they found after intervention for one school year, the only approach achieving average reading proficiency levels was direct instruction. They even found no improvements for many children taught using context-based approaches. They concluded the influence of curriculum was stronger than the influences of different teachers and of tutoring. Studies also find that while students require skills in phonological analysis and decoding to read successfully, these alone are insufficient. Students must additionally develop the ability for rapid decoding of words that demonstrate the orthographic components of our language, such as morphological units (the smallest grammatical units conveying different meanings) and writing conventions. Students must also be taught individual comprehension processes. Reading skills are affected by literacy immersion, print awareness, and being read to, but do not predict long-term reading success as strongly as single-word skills.

Example of an informal reading assessment to assess print concepts awareness

To assess a student's awareness of print concepts 1:1, a teacher should arrange for a quiet, comfortable setting without distractions. Ideally, another teacher or aide can supervise the class in working quietly while the assessing teacher sits in a quiet corner with one student. The teacher should have a simple checklist, with each task listed and Yes/No columns to check for each task the student can/cannot complete successfully. Teachers can complete this checklist several times per school year, periodically repeating tasks the student did not succeed at until s/he can do so. The teacher gives the student a storybook and asks him/her to demonstrate the following: Recognize the book's front; recognize the book's back; identify the book's title; identify a word on/in the book; identify a letter in a word in the book; identify a space between words in the book; identify the place where the teacher should start reading the book aloud; and identify a period as the punctuation mark ending a sentence.

Example of an informal reading assessment that a teacher can use 1:1 to test recognition of rhyming

When informally assessing a child's ability to identify rhymes, the teacher first asks the child whether s/he knows what rhyming words are. If the child answers "Yes," the teacher then asks the child to supply two words that rhyme. If the child answers "No," or says "Yes" but gives a non-rhyming example, the teacher explains that rhyming words end with the same sound and gives an example, like hat and cat. The teacher tells the student, "I'm going to say two words; I want you to tell me if they sound the same at the end." The teacher uses a simple checklist. Each item will list the two words presented, with places for Correct or Incorrect to check or circle indicating the child's answer. The actual word pairs used should always be written/printed to help identify problem areas with specific sounds. For example, if the teacher presents bag and tag, the child should say "Yes." But if the teacher presents bag and bun, the child should respond "No."

Conducting an informal classroom assessment of literacy skill for identifying initial word sounds

To conduct informal individual assessments of student ability to identify word-initial phonemes, the teacher first gives an example, such as, "Some words start with the same sound, like fun and fat both start with /f/." The teacher then says, "I'm going to say two words. I want you to tell me if they start with the same sound. Let's try one: Do the words boat and box start with the same sound?" The teacher uses a simple checklist. Numbering each word pair presented, the teacher marks each of the student's answers correct/incorrect. It is important to write the actual words used, to facilitate identifying patterns of difficulty a student might have with certain sounds for remediation via direct instruction. This can also sometimes reveal undiagnosed hearing impairments or auditory processing disorders. The teacher presents correct pairs like pig and pen, and incorrect pairs like hat and man. Teachers can periodically repeat this assessment to monitor progress, and use the results to target specific problem phonemes for remediation.

Testing a student's ability to blend words and segment phonemes as literacy skills

For assessing blending, the teacher tells the student, "Let's play 'Guess My Word.' I'm going to say a word, but I'm going to say it in parts. I want you to guess what the word is. Here's an example: /c/--/at/." Can you guess the word?" The teacher uses a simple, numbered checklist. For each numbered item, the teacher has pre-written/printed the two sounds to present, such as /s/ and /un/, /b/ and /all/, etc. The teacher marks the student's response to each item as Correct or Incorrect. For phoneme segmentation, the teacher says, "I'm going to say a word. I want you to separate the word into the different sounds you hear. Let's practice: If I say 'cat,' you would say, /c/-/a/-/t/." The teacher presents a series of one-syllable words, which s/he has pre-written/printed on a checklist similar to the blending checklist, and marks the student's responses as correct/incorrect. Both assessments can be repeated periodically. Teachers can also analyze student responses for specific problem areas to remediate.

Conducting an informal 1:1 classroom assessment of literacy skills for phoneme manipulation and deletion

For phonemic manipulation skills, the teacher can tell the student that in the word game they will play, "I'll say a word. I want you to change the word's first sound to /s/. Let's practice first. If I said cat, then you would say sat." The teacher has written a series of such simple, monosyllabic words on a numbered checklist, with the correct answer next to each, and lines/boxes/columns next to that to mark the student response as Correct or Incorrect. For example, the correct response in this example for run would be sun. For phoneme deletion, the teacher tells the student, "I'll say a word. I want you to say it without the first sound. Let's practice: If I said fun, you would say un." The teacher then presents a series of similar short words pre-written/printed on a checklist like the one for phoneme manipulation, with the correct answers and places to mark student responses Correct/Incorrect. Teachers can re-use these assessments to monitor student progress.

Running records

Teachers can assess a student's current reading performance by taking running records as the student reads aloud. For purposes of conducting running record assessments, some books have been selected for use, called benchmark books. These are published with accompanying running record forms, with text excerpts from the books pre-printed on them. The first 100-150 words of a benchmark book are typically used for running records in higher grades. For teachers wanting to use more text, or different books, publishers also provide blank forms. The teacher annotates the form with marks showing correct and incorrect word reading; error types, such as omission, insertion, substitution, or repetition; self-corrections; saying a word's initial phoneme first; and interventions. Teachers also can note, if desired, the types of cues—meaning, structural, and visual—the student uses, to analyze student reading behavior and gain deeper understanding of reading problems, as applicable. Experts consider unfamiliar grade-level fiction and nonfiction books more accurate indices of student reading ability. Teachers may use familiar texts for some students if they prefer.

Experts recommend early emergent readers be assessed with running records of their reading every 2-4 weeks; emergent readers every 4-6 weeks; early fluent readers every 6-8 weeks; and fluent readers every 8-10 weeks. Teachers pick a book close to the student's reading level, telling the student to read aloud as the teacher observes and records notes. The teacher sits alongside the student to view text and student eye and finger movements. The teacher check-marks each correctly read word. If the student reads a word incorrectly, the teacher writes above that word what the student read. If a student reads too rapidly for teacher recording, the teacher asks him/her to pause until the teacher has caught up the recording. Teachers attend to reader behavior, like whether s/he is using visual, structural, and/or meaning cues for decoding and comprehension. Teachers make minimal interruptions/interventions. If the student gets stuck on a word, teachers wait 5-10 seconds and then, say the word. If the student is confused, explain and have him/her try again.

On the running record form, the teacher places a check-mark above every word read correctly. Word substitutions without self-correction count as one error regardless of number; the teacher writes the substitution(s) above the word. The teacher places a long dash above any word the student omits. If the student inserts an extra word, the teacher marks the location with a caret, writing the inserted word above it. Word repetitions are marked R; two repetitions are R2, three repetitions R3. Phrase repetitions are marked R with an arrow pointing to where the repetition began. Marking SC following an error denotes student self-correction. If the teacher must intervene, saying "Try again," s/he brackets the problematic text, marking TA above. If the teacher must intervene, telling the student a word after 5-10 seconds, s/he marks a T above the word. If the student says a word's initial sound first, the teacher marks that initial sound above the word, following with a check-mark if the student then says the word.

When a student considers the background of a story or other text s/he reads aloud; the information in text illustrations; and/or what particular sentences mean, s/he is using meaning cues. When the teacher observes this reading behavior, s/he marks M on the running record form. When the student uses his/her implicit knowledge of sentence structure and syntax to determine whether his/her reading sounds right, this is using structural cues; teachers mark S. Observing word-initial letters/sounds, letters' and words' appearances, word lengths, familiar phrases, etc., constitutes using visual cues; teachers mark V. The teacher's first step is checking correctly read words and marking errors on the form. Teachers should first familiarize themselves with the symbols and marking conventions used. It also helps to practice with another teacher who plays the role of the student reading aloud and purposely makes errors to record. The second step, based on the first step's markings, is filling the form's boxes for each sentence/line read: number of errors, self-corrections, and M/S/V cues used for each error/self-correction.

After recording correctly read words, errors and error types, etc., the teacher totals the student's number of errors and self-corrections. To calculate the student's error rate, divide the total number of words read by the total number of errors made. The ratio errors: words expresses how many words were read correctly per error; for example, 100 words read/10 errors = 1:10, meaning that for each error, the student read 10 words correctly. The formula for accuracy rate, expressed as a percentage, is total words read minus total errors, divided by total words read; for instance, (100 words – 10 errors)/100 = 90/100 = 0.90 = 90% accuracy. This rate can be compared against text difficulty: Independent-level reading = 95-100% accuracy rate; Instructional-level = 90-94%; and Frustration-level = 89% or lower. Self-correction rate, expressed as a ratio, is calculated with the formula (Number of errors + number of self-corrections)/number of self-corrections; for example, (10 + 5)/5 = 15/5 = 3; self-correction rate = 1:3, or 1 self-correction for every 3 errors. Self-correction rates of 1:4 or lower show that students are self-monitoring their reading.

In addition to quantitatively calculating a student's accuracy rate, error rate, and self-correction rate, a teacher can also make a qualitative analysis of the student's reading development through taking a running record of the student reading aloud. While taking the running record, the teacher has observed the student's reading behaviors and marked whenever s/he observed the student using visual (V), structural (S), and/or meaning (M) cues to help decode and comprehend what s/he read aloud. In addition to how the student used these cues, the teacher has also paid attention to the student's reading fluency, phrasing, and intonational patterns while reading aloud. Moreover, using the notations s/he made and his/her memory of the reading, the teacher considers what kinds of prompts s/he gave to help the student when needed and how the student responded to each prompt and prompt type. Combining all these observations informs the teacher's qualitative analysis of the student's reading to formulate an overall picture of student reading development.

Miscue analysis

K. S. Goodman (1969) developed and named the approach of miscue analysis, which is used to examine a reader's specific strategies. Wrong guesses, i.e. miscues, made by a student when reading a text aloud, contain information that can inform the listener/teacher as to how hard/easy the student finds the text to read; and how unfamiliar/familiar the student is with the text's content. This information gained from analyzing miscues is not available from standard reading test results, because reading entails far more than simply examining every letter and word closely. Goodman identified three cueing systems as foundations of the reading process: (1) letter-to-sound relationships, i.e. the **grapho/phonic** cueing system; (2) sentence structure, word order, and grammar—i.e. the **syntactic** cueing system; and (3) the meanings we recognize from words, i.e. the **semantic** cueing system. Goodman proposed that patterns in a reader's miscues/mistakes reveal both weaknesses and strengths; and that through these miscues, combined with what s/he can describe about how s/he made them, we can understand the learner's reading process.

Miscue analysis (Goodman, 1969) focuses on the types of errors readers make for information about the learner's reading skills and strategies. For example, substituting "the machine's performance" for text "the machine's programming"; "reading for instructions" for "ready for instructions"; "hadn't changed" for "hated changes"; "clean" for "clear", but then corrects this; and immediately self-corrects "found" to "fond", has substituted noun for noun, adjective for adjective, and verb form for verb form. S/he has substituted words resembling the correct ones, not drastically changing the meaning. The reader also self-corrected as soon as s/he found that certain errors made no sense in context. This reader reads for meaning by using all three cueing systems—grapho/phonic, or how words look; semantic, or what words mean; and syntactic, or how words sound and are organized. Conversely, a reader who substitutes "dropped on" with "dropping from"; "planes" with "plans"; "horses" with "arches"; "really" with "already"; "more" with "move"; "to" with "the"; and "cinema" with "camera" substitutes mostly similar-looking words, disregarding the meaning.

Using miscue analysis can show differential reading proficiency in different students, but not from counting each student's miscues/errors. For example, two students might make the same number of reading errors; but by analyzing their miscues, we discover one seeks meaning while reading, whereas the other seeks simply to complete the reading whether it makes sense or not. One reader substitutes incorrect words very similar in appearance, sound, and meaning to the correct ones, and/or self-corrects misread words when they make no sense in context. This student reads for meaning. The other reader substitutes incorrect words that look similar to the correct ones, but are grammatically wrong and/or have no meaning in their context. Such a reader may also decode as s/he reads, or read word-for-word. This student does not read for meaning. One strategy is using a cloze procedure, i.e. short passages with gaps to fill. This helps the student focusing mainly on letter/word appearances to predict also the contextual, semantic cues and syntactic, grammatical cues that facilitate finding meaning.

Experts caution that beginning readers are not good candidates for the use of miscue analysis as a reading assessment. Early readers may not have developed an understanding of phonics sufficient for decoding printed language and must depend completely on semantic (meaning) cues in text. Additionally, researchers find students with inadequate reading skills rely less on contextual cues for reading comprehension and fluency; so miscue

- 66 -

analysis would yield little useful information about their reading either. When miscue analysis is appropriate, experts recommend giving students a choice of 3-4 texts. Fewer can prevent students from selecting text they prefer; more can be overwhelming. In general, guidelines are to give students at lower (applicable) entry reading levels passages of around 100 words or so; around 200 words at upper entry levels; and longer selections at higher reading levels. Assessing educators should secure about 30 minutes in a quiet room without interruptions (including ringing phones); good lighting; a recorder with good sound quality; and clear copies of text for reading and scoring.

The three cueing systems identified by Goodman (1969) in his method of miscue analysis are grapho/phonic, semantic, and syntactic. In the grapho/phonic cueing system, the appearances of words are their salient features. A student who makes miscues (errors) that have effective grapho/phonic similarities might substitute the word "owning" for the text word "owing"; "strengthened" for "straightened"; "determent" for "detriment"; and/or "wrist" for "waist". Here the miscued words are very similar in shape, length, and meaning to the text words. Miscues with partial grapho/phonic similarities include mistaking "fortitude" for "fortunate"; "present" for "patient"; "acclimatization" for "accumulation"; and/or "sedately" for "sadly". These differ more in appearance and meaning than those with effective similarities (above). Miscues having little or no grapho/phonic similarity include mistaking "usual" for "surface"; "present" for "perched"; "flickering" for "blinking"; and/or "almost" for "awfully". The less similarity between the text's original word and the reader's miscue, the more likely the text author's intention will be lost or misconstrued, and the less likely the reader will comprehend the text's meaning.

Miscue analysis focuses on the three cueing systems identified by its author Goodman (1969): grapho/phonic, semantic, and syntactic. In the semantic system, meaning is the key factor. When reading aloud, the errors/miscues a student makes can vary in how semantically strong they are, i.e. how much they affect the text's meaning. When a student's miscues do not alter the text author's meaning significantly, they are viewed as having high semantic strength and acceptability. For example, the student might read "destructive" instead of "disruptive," volcanic" instead of "violent," or "offer" instead of "afford". Miscues with partial semantic acceptability or strength seem suitable within one phrase, clause, or sentence but not the text's overall context. These include, for example, reading "horse" for "house"; "penguins" for "pigeons"; "special" for "species"; or "regarded" for "rewarded". Miscues with poor semantic strength include reading "pigments" for "pigeons"; "parent" for "present"; or "over" for "owner". These are less acceptable because the miscues share less meaning with the original words in the text.

To assess reading problems, miscue analysis (Goodman, 1969) divides reading into three coding or cueing systems: grapho/phonic, semantic, and syntactic. The syntactic cueing system supplies information about whether words/phrases/clauses function grammatically within the context of their sentences. A student may misread some words orally, yet demonstrate the recognition that the incorrect words fit the sentence's syntax as well as the text's original words. For example, syntactically strong miscues include these: misreading text that says "He had huge arms" as "He had huge hands"; misreading "It was fully mature" as "It was finally mature"; or misreading "...to send her as a present" as "...to send her as a patient". These incorrect words still fit the sentences' grammatical contexts. Syntactically weak miscues, by contrast, include reading "...both sides of his face" as "...besides of his face"; "He was completely devoid of hair" as "He was completely devote of hair"; or "...a glitter of ironic laughter" as "...a greater of ironic laughter". These substitutions are grammatically as well as semantically incorrect.

Miscue analysis classifies reading errors into different categories, e.g., insertion, substitution, omission, repetition, reversal, hesitation, and self-correction. One such category is non-response. According to miscue analysis (Goodman, 1969), a student who fails to respond lacks understanding of the grapho/phonic (letter-to-sound) system, limiting his/her word-attack skills. The student uses sight words, limiting his/her attack to the visual modality without accompanying sound/phonic information. Students who fail to respond upon encountering unknown words are afraid to guess, so they likely also do not avail themselves of contextual cues. They are also characterized as anxious readers who do not want to experience public "failure." The teacher should ask the student whether s/he attempts to decipher unknown words by: analyzing letter-to-sound relationships; identifying letter clusters and syllables within a word; identifying smaller words contained within larger words; using visual analogies (e.g., "hard" looks like "card"); using the syntax to predict likely word choices; and/or using the content to predict likely words. This questioning reveals what processes occur in the student upon encountering unknown words.

According to miscue analysis of reading (Goodman, 1969), if a student misreads some words, but the words s/he substitutes have similar appearances, sounds, and meanings to the original text words, this may suggest that the student is attacking the text impulsively and/or hurriedly. The solution is to encourage the student to slow down a little when reading. However, if the student makes errors by substituting words very different from the original text, s/he is likely to have poor skills in the grapho/phonic cueing system—i.e. poor knowledge or understanding of letter-to-sound relationships—and in addition is not compensating for these by using the surrounding sentence and passage context to predict what word(s) are likely in that context. Direct instruction in grapho-phonemic relationships, and in attending to context, are indicated. If a student's miscues involve familiar, common, and small words, this can show that the student's sight vocabulary is weak and needs further development through intensive instruction and practice.

According to Goodman's (1969) miscue analysis, one reason some students insert extraneous words into the text they read aloud is that they are attracted to the future word(s) in a sentence and are prematurely trying to incorporate it to their sense of semantic acceptability—that is, have it make sense in context in terms of meaning. Another factor to consider is that readers fluent enough not to read one word at a time might be reading a bit too quickly, leading to insertion miscues. The author cautions the teacher not to over-emphasize such student insertion errors if they do not significantly alter the meaning of the text. However, at the same time, the teacher must consider whether the student's insertion miscues are syntactic in nature (for example, morphological insertions like changing the word "full" to the word "fully"), because such structural additions can change the sentence meaning. When this is the case, the teacher needs to point out to the student the differences in meaning produced by the insertion.

According to the miscue analysis model (Goodman, 1969), miscues/errors involving word omission can be made by a student who reads a little bit faster than his or her proficiency allows for accuracy. Omissions can also occur when the reader has a weak sight word vocabulary. When leaving out small and regular words does not change the meaning of the text, teachers can overlook these student oversights. However, it is important for teachers to remember how the meaning of a sentence, clause, or phrase can be changed—indeed, completely reversed—when the reader omits such a word as "not". Teachers should observe whether the student consistently or frequently omits entire lines rather than just single words: omission of whole lines can indicate poor skills with eye tracking. This can sometimes also indicate additional problems, such as visual field defects interrupt and/or truncate eye tracking. For further analysis, teachers should also observe where students omit words: before unfamiliar/challenging words; in the middle of passages; and/or at the ends of lines.

According to miscue analysis, good readers search for meaning in text and seek to consolidate meaning; therefore, some repetitions indicate good reading skills/strategies. However, if a student repeats too often, the text may be too difficult, sacrificing fluency to attain comprehension. In addition to adjusting text difficulty levels, teachers should observe whether a student repeats just before a harder word; this can indicate the student is stalling for time in order to decode it. Similarly to repetitions, corrections also demonstrate awareness of the text's meaning in good readers. However, overly frequent self-corrections can mean the student is reading a bit too rapidly. They can also mean the reader is responding to the visual shapes of words prematurely to considering their meanings. Excessive self-corrections can compromise the student's reading comprehension, even when corrections do not change the text meaning. Another consideration is that students who do not perceive themselves as good readers may correct their reading even when it was already accurate.

According to miscue analysis, students may reverse words or phrases in a sentence without affecting the text's overall meaning, in which case the author (Goodman, 1969) finds little cause for concern. However, the author also points out that some word and phrase reversals will change the syntax or grammar of the sentence. The student's response to this altered word order and sentence structure can often be to try to make up for the change in the sentence's sequence of ideas by forcing alternative verb endings and other such morphological changes. At times when a student reverses letters within a single word, such as reading "saw" for "was", this will not substantially affect the meaning of the sentence; however, at other times it will do so, such as reading "no" instead of "on". Research finds that students are likely to make such reversals more frequently with short words that are used most often (i.e., "high-frequency" words) in printed text.

According to Goodman (1969)'s miscue analysis model, students who do not perceive themselves as good reader tend to hesitate when reading aloud due to lack of self-confidence. Students with weak visual skills are more likely to hesitate. Students with deficient grapho/phonic skills, i.e. understanding and applying the relationships of written letters to spoken sounds, are also more likely to hesitate during reading aloud. Another factor contributing to reading hesitation is text difficulty. While in some cases the teacher can provide less challenging text, in many cases—especially in secondary school grades—content-area courses require the reading of specified texts, making it inevitable that some students read some texts too difficult for their individual reading skills. Teachers can glean further information about the student's reading behavior by observing where s/he hesitates in reading. Always hesitating before unknown/challenging words indicates the student knows and is preparing for what is coming. Always hesitating at the beginnings/ends of lines may reveal the student has difficulties with smoothly eye-tracking the text.

Miscue analysis finds student Alex attempts every word in the text; comprehends the text's main meanings; recognizes punctuation; and makes some self-corrections. That many of Alex's substitution errors use visually similar words—of similar length and shape, with the same initial letters—indicate his primary word-recognition strategies are visual. Alex also sometimes uses semantic cues, i.e. meaning in the text, to decipher words, evidenced by substituting words he knows for similar, unfamiliar ones. However, he sometimes also misreads words/phrases with substitutions making no sense. Alex's knowledge of letter-to-sound relationships is shaky; for this reason, he does not effectively apply decoding strategies to new words. He reads words holistically without closely analyzing their components and, for this reason, he omits suffixes, plural endings, etc. This changes the grammar, so he must then change subsequent words to fit. Instruction in advance text scanning, analyzing word features and meanings, and discussing possible text content can increase his reading comprehension and fluency.

Observations a teacher should record about a student's reading aloud

In addition to recording which words were omitted; which substituted and with what; which words were inserted; and words where the reader does not respond, the teacher should also observe the following reader behaviors in the student: Whether or not the student reads one word at a time; if the student reads aloud in a jerky manner; if the student uses inappropriate or absent intonational variations; whether the student misses lines while reading and/or loses his/her place in the text; whether the student observes punctuation in the text when reading aloud, or fails to pause and to change pitch, etc., accordingly with punctuation marks; whether the student places vocal stress on each and every syllable; whether the student reads fluently, hesitating only before challenging words, or reads hesitantly overall; whether or not the student pauses after phrases/clauses and sentences; and most of all, whether the student comprehends the meaning of the overall text or not. The teacher should record Yes/No to these based on observations of the student reading aloud.

Student self-evaluations of reading progress

When students at any reading level have no idea yet how to use fundamental reading strategies, such as phonemic awareness or the alphabetic principle, to decode printed language, they are likely not ready for self-evaluation, let alone applying it to remedial efforts. However, once any student has gained some experience with attempting to read aloud and receiving evaluations and corrections from a teacher, the teacher can introduce the student to principles and practices of self-evaluation, and the self-correction it informs. Very young beginning readers are in earlier stages of cognitive development and often cannot view/analyze their reading processes objectively. However, teachers can instruct them in simpler, more concrete self-evaluations, such as identifying their errors as they read aloud. Teachers begin by correcting younger students, and then gradually introducing questions and directions guiding them to identify all individual letters in a word; sound out the word; decide whether their reading of a word makes sense in the context, etc. Students will eventually internalize these practices as self-monitoring habits, improving their literacy skills.

Anecdotal records

Anecdotal records cannot replace formal/informal reading tests/inventories or other assessment instruments, but can provide valuable supplements to these. For example, whenever a teacher, teacher's aide, specialist, therapist, or other personnel who interact with students during reading-related activities notices a specific student reading behavior, or a recurring pattern in the student's reading behaviors, s/he can record it by simply writing down an account of what s/he observed. Personnel other than the student's teacher should share this information with the teacher, who can also include it in the student's records after reviewing and considering it. Anecdotal records differ from other assessment instruments in that they do not involve quantitative measurements, such as computing all numbers of errors, error types, etc. Anecdotal records do not require statistical proof of validity or reliability, or compare student performance to a norm or a criterion. An anecdote is simply a narrative description of an event or incident. Educators can often glean important clues about student reading problems/behaviors from analyzing anecdotal reports after they are made.

Curriculum-Based Measurement (CBM)

CBM furnishes methods to assess academic proficiency in reading, as well as in writing, spelling, and math. Whereas traditional assessments measure skills mastery, CBM focuses on fluency, and reflects changes in both response ease and accuracy in its scoring. Also, each score in CBM reflects overall proficiency in each academic subject. For example, CBM uses fluency in reading passages as a measure of overall reading proficiency because passage reading demands coordinating multi-dimensional reading skills like word recognition, decoding, and comprehension. CBM also affords modeling of academic improvement within a school year: Educators plot individual scores of regular weekly/monthly/quarterly CBM administrations on graphs, representing student progress rates as slopes. They connect a year-end goal, representing NCLB's AYP requirement, to a student's beginning CBM score, to create a goal line showing the desired improvement rate. When student scores drop below the goal line, teachers find their existing teaching programs insufficient, and adjust them toward increasing student learning rates.

Accessing literacy research and applying it across grade levels

Today, educators, students, and parents can avail themselves of a wealth of resources to access research into literacy development, especially online. For example, the website and company Education Planet offers a database containing over 100,000 instructional resources, e-learning services, and web tools approved by teachers. Teachers can use this site to share instructional ideas and experiences, learn additional ways to integrate technology into their curricula, and search more than 16,000 lesson plans. Education World's search engine can be filtered to search only educational websites. Education World also includes information on best classroom technology applications, lesson plans, educational experts' articles, education-related news items, website reviews, and job listings. Educators can search one million-plus records of educational theory, research, and practice in the ERIC Database via the Educator's Reference Desk website, as well as over 2,000 lesson plans, archives of 200+ question answers, and 3,000+ links to education information online. A website established by educators for disseminating educational information and resources, and offering free services to educators and students, is GreatTeacher.net.

Supporting school-wide reading initiatives that focus on assessment of reading

School administrators and other members of leadership should endeavor to learn as much as they can about the formative assessment(s) their school uses. Formative assessments reflect ongoing learning rather than what has been learned by end-of-lesson/unit/semester/year, which is measured by summative assessments. School leaders should learn how to gather data within their school's formative assessment system, and use this knowledge to help educators by periodically collecting data themselves. Members of leadership should also learn how to read and interpret the information in their data reports, and how to apply it to direct their school's instruction. They should also use the information in data reports for guiding regular planning meetings for each grade level in their school. To provide leadership in the area of reading assessment, they should also regularly engage in conversations with teachers about data collected regarding their students' performance in reading, discussing ideas with them for fine-tuning their instruction to make it most effective.

Standards produced by the No Child Left Behind (NCLB) Act

Since NCLB was enacted, educators have pursued increased interest in measuring and improving student learning through standards-based assessments. At first, educators concentrated on yearly, state-level standardized test results. However, they soon discovered that these findings were "too little, too late" for identifying students lagging behind grade/peer levels. But they discovered concurrently that classroom-level formative assessments could achieve statistically significant student learning progress. Experts identify benchmark assessment as the middle ground between state-level and classroom-level formative assessment. Benchmarks assessments are made at certain times during a curriculum sequence, throughout school years. They assess student skills and knowledge related to a specified group of long-term learning goals. The expected users of benchmark assessments, the purposes for their uses, and how the assessment instruments are used dictate the selection and design of benchmark assessments. These benchmark assessments can inform instructional planning, decisions at classroom/school/district levels, and educational policy.

Instruction in generating rhymes for ELL students and special-needs students

Teachers can teach students to recognize rhymes and generate their own rhymes through explicit instruction in manipulating the onsets (word-initial phonemes) and rimes (stems) of words, supplementing oral practice with visual graphics. Research findings verify that explicit instruction in phonemic awareness is helpful to English language learners (ELLs). To deliver such explicit training to ELL students, teachers may need to provide scaffolding, i.e., temporary support they gradually decrease as student proficiency increases for their comprehension of English rhyming words. Teachers can use pictures representing words, and have ELL students sort them into groups that rhyme, like *cat* with *mat.* Teachers can also use this activity to assess ELL students' oral vocabulary comprehension and phonemic awareness skills in English. For special-needs students, teachers can use magnetized letters with bumps, providing visual and tactile stimuli. This gives special-needs students multisensory materials for augmented support for manipulating word parts and generating new rhyming words, and for transferring their phonemic awareness skills to reading activities.

Instruction in phonemic awareness via multisensory mapping activities for ELL and special-needs students

Teachers can help first-grade students develop phonological processing skills by providing explicit instruction using multiple sensory modalities, aiding comprehension and retention. Technology provides differentiation for ELL students using technology. For example, ELL students view printed words in onscreen text, type in rhyming words, and listen to stories or songs accompanying the text. There are websites offering activities for word-building. For example, www.readwritethink.org features interactive activities like "Construct a Word," wherein ELL students can find rhyming words, generate matching rhymes, and receive feedback and scores on their responses. Teachers can follow this activity by providing ELL students with repeated reading practice via a podcast and accompanying word sheet of paired rhyming words that the site also supplies. Multisensory modalities and repeated exposures also benefit special-needs students. Teachers can differentiate instruction for them by playing a podcast song like "Old MacDonald" for wordplay and rhyme generation and having students make flip-books with pictures of animals illustrating rhyming words and color-coded text. For ongoing practice, students can even trade their flip books with classmates.

Phonemic awareness instructional activity of matching picture cards to phonemes for ELL and special-needs students

Identifying and classifying phonemes that are word-initial, word-medial, or word-final can be particularly challenging for students learning English as a new language. When they use picture cards in a matching game for identifying phonemes, teachers can differentiate it for additional support to ELL students by adding "sound boxes." Teachers prompt ELL students to identify how many phonemes are in a word, then put one token per sound into corresponding boxes, and then find a picture card of something starting with each sound. This gives ELL students concrete visual aids for sound and phoneme identification and classification. Studies show special-needs students also improve their reading significantly through systematic, explicit phonemic awareness instruction. Using multisensory modalities helps them process and recall phonemes. Teachers can differentiate instruction by giving them cued signals for phonemes. For example, teachers have students put their hands in front of their mouths when producing vocalized phonemes or watch their mouth shapes in mirrors while producing specific phonemes. Involving touch and movement promotes their processing and mapping of speech sounds.

Sound-sorting instructional activities

Studies find that systematic, explicit instruction in phonemic awareness, like sound-sorting activities, benefit students learning English as a second language (ESL) by teaching them to focus on specific speech sounds. When teachers have students sort picture cards according to the word position of target phonemes, they can differentiate this instruction for ESL students by analyzing each student's assessment results and making individualized packages of picture cards for them with numbers on the backs for self-correction that focus on whichever phonemes each student needs to practice. Teachers can also make podcasts giving word labels for each picture and prompts for classifying each sound. As ESL student proficiency in phoneme classification increases, teachers can gradually withdraw podcasts. Deficient phonemic awareness and phonological processing also puts special-needs students at risk of failing at reading. Teachers can differentiate sound-sorting for them by adding picture cards with tactile surfaces and/or having students write letters in substrates like sand or cornmeal while repeating the sounds aloud.

Instructional activity using sound-play targeting segmenting and blending phonemes

Teachers can help develop phonological and phonemic awareness skills by providing them with games involving systematic, explicit instruction in separating and combining phonemes in words. This teaches the decoding skills necessary for reading. Teachers can differentiate these activities, like a "Treasure Chest" activity using picture cards, pennies, and a Treasure Chest board or sheet, for ELL students by additionally making them a computer podcast giving the names for each picture card. In the podcast, the teacher (or whoever is speaking in the recording) also separates these words into their component phonemes and blends the individual phonemes into words. Students learning English as a new language need repeated phonemic practice. They receive supplementary support by using the picture cards while listening to the podcast as an in-class activity and/or homework. Special-needs students also get more practice by playing a guessing game with this activity: in pairs, they take turns, one giving the other clues to the names for each picture card and the other guessing using segmented words (e.g., "/d/o/g/").

Assessing phonemic awareness according to specific phonemic awareness skills

Experts often use three levels of performance for phonemic awareness skills: Beginning, Developing, and Proficient. To assess young students' skill levels, educators can give them phonemic awareness tasks targeting specific skills, observe their responses, and evaluate their performance as corresponding to one of these levels. Specific skills include: recognizing rhymes, generating rhymes, identifying phonemes, manipulating phonemes, blending phonemes, and segmenting phonemes. For each of these specific skill areas, a student at the Beginning level will only *rarely* demonstrate the skill; for example, the student only rarely identifies words that rhyme; rarely generates words that rhyme; rarely identifies selected phonemes; rarely manipulates the positions of phonemes in a word among initial, medial, or final; rarely blends phonemes to produce words; and rarely segments words into their separate component phonemes. At the Developing level, students will *sometimes* demonstrate these skills. At the Proficient level, students will *always* demonstrate these skills.

Assessing student skills in the alphabetic principle

Elementary school students must receive systematic, explicit instruction in letter-sound correspondences beginning immediately in kindergarten if not sooner in order to develop the reading skills they will need in future grades. This includes being able to recite the alphabet; being able to identify all alphabet letters, including upper-case, lower-case, and cursive forms by their appearance; being able to connect the speech sounds they hear to the correct alphabet letters that represent them; and reciprocally, being able to see alphabet letters and produce the correct speech sounds that the letters represent. Students in the early elementary grades must gain these and other skills that are prerequisite to developing reading skills, including accuracy and fluency, that will enable them to read printed text on their respective grade levels with good comprehension. For elementary school students to meet the expectations of their teachers and schools, including expectations mandated by federal laws and aligned state and local laws, schools should assess student learning not only by the particular curriculum, but by grade-level benchmarks.

Assessment results to instructional design for pre-reading and reading skills

Educators must collect assessment data on each of their individual students. They obtain these data by administering various standardized tests; informal assessments; progress monitoring measures included in their curricula; and daily measurements of student performance and progress, including observations and observational checklists as well as written quizzes, tests, and homework assignments. Educators must then analyze the data they gather to identify patterns in each student's learning needs. Once they have identified such patterns, teachers must focus their instruction to target their remediation. Their teaching activities must include: systematic, explicit instruction based on research evidence of effective teaching practices in skills which the students have not learned yet; how to apply those skills once they have learned them; and ample, repeated practice in applying those skills, which should be spread over sufficient periods of time. Teachers must also use assessments on an ongoing basis to monitor student progress and detect deficits in pre-reading and reading skills. They must then re-teach those skills found deficient, and reassess student learning after re-teaching.

Evaluating the letter knowledge of a student at the emergent reading level

Teachers need to assess young students' pre-reading and reading skills to determine their knowledge levels to know which skills to teach and deficits to address, to identify error patterns and focus on remediating them, and even on which individual phonemes and/or letters they need to focus on learning. To assess letter knowledge, the teacher must evaluate all of its elements systematically. If the teacher has the student sing the Alphabet Song, this only shows successful memorization, not letter knowledge. Having the student list alphabet letters he or she knows is not systematic, and does not address all aspects of letter knowledge. Presenting letters visually is better, but if the teacher only has the student sound these out, this again does not assess all components of letter knowledge. The best method would be presenting letters visually and having the student name them. This addresses the student's letter recognition, knowledge of letter names, and ability to differentiate among letters, which are all elements included in letter knowledge.

Whole-group phonics instruction

In the LEAD21 (Wright Group, 2010-2013) model of phonics instruction, teachers begin each day with a warm-up activity in phonemic awareness. They provide students with sound-spelling cards and introduce decodable readers to them on the first day. They also introduce the week's spelling list and give the spelling pre-test for that list on day one. On the first and third days, students use sound-spelling cards. Teachers show them example words and model phoneme blending. Students then practice blending, first in isolation and then within context, using high-frequency words. On the second and fourth days, classes review the blending skill, and practice isolated and contextual blending again. They also build words and review word patterns using high-frequency words, and reread the decodable readers on days two and four. The students practice spelling on days two, three, and four. Teachers introduce a new word study skill on day two, and review this skill with the class on day four. Teachers give the class the week's spelling post-test on day five.

Teachers using the LEAD21 model from the Wright Group with second-grade classes introduce their students to a new component of phonics on the first weekday. On the third day, they review the new component introduced the previous week. Teachers give students time to conduct inquiry projects on the fifth weekday. The first three weeks of the month involve teaching new phonics components. During the fourth week of the month, teachers do not introduce any more new items, but review everything they taught the previous three weeks. Whole-class activities are interactive. This model includes scaffolding (graduated support) that enables all students to take part in the activities. The model also allows teachers to conduct brief reviews with small student groups, and follow up whole-class lessons with literacy stations where individual student needs and practice are addressed. Whole-class instruction includes weekly spelling lists and tests, and word study activities. Each phonics and word study skill has a *"Phonics Companion"* page for independent student completion.

Procedure for differentiating reading fluency instruction for various students in a class

One expert (Pennington, 2009) outlines a way to differentiate reading fluency instruction. After assessing students' fluency and assigning them to small groups based on reading levels and fluency rates, teachers have each student make his or her own fluency folder. Many fluency bar graphs are available online; teachers select graphs appropriate for student fluency speed, give each student a graph for his or her folder, and collect the folders. They assign "Fluency Leaders" for each group who collect and turn in group materials and ask the teacher questions or request assistance on their group's behalf. Teachers should tell the groups they will get incentives for participation and for making transitions quickly, cooperatively, and quietly. Teachers instruct groups to read aloud softly for two-minute "cold" readings, or readings performed without practice or preparation. Then they show students how to tally word counts and record their scores on their bar graphs. After the cold reading, teachers instruct students to continue where they left off and repeatedly reread their passages until the teacher gets to their group.

Reading specialist Mark Pennington (2009) advises teachers in a procedure for differentiated reading fluency instruction in a classroom. After a teacher has assessed students' fluency and assigned them to small groups according to their reading levels and fluency rates, had them do an unpracticed two-minute reading, tallied the words per minute they have read, recorded their scores on fluency bar graphs, and then practiced repeatedly, the teacher then visits each group, starting with the group with the lowest reading fluency. They pre-teach the group a few "challenging" words from the text by saying them and having students repeat, also giving short definitions if needed to inform passage meaning. They then lead the group in reading the passage aloud together, modeling correct pronunciation and expression. A "challenge" speed for modeling is around 30 percent faster than the speed of the group's slowest reader. Once the group is reading aloud at the required speed, the teacher reads in a quieter voice.

A reading expert (Pennington, 2009) has defined a procedure to help teachers differentiate their class instruction in reading fluency. The teacher has divided students into small groups based on reading levels and fluency rates, and taught them to do short "cold" (unpracticed) readings of a passage, tally their words per minute, and record their scores on fluency bar graphs provided. The teacher has visited each group and led them in choral readings, modeling a faster reading rate. Once students attain this rate, the teacher assigns the group's Fluency Leader to take the teacher's place while he or she moves to another group. Groups reread the entire passage aloud together. The teacher has students reread the passage individually as rapidly as they feel able. Once the last group finishes both choral readings, the teacher has students do a "hot" (or practiced) reading of the passage, tally words per minute and record these on the graphs. The graphs then show the difference in students' speed between the "cold" and "hot" readings.

Differentiating instruction in reading fluency

When instructing students in reading fluency, experts advise dividing them into small groups based on similar reading levels and fluency rates. They recommend that teachers work with students on attending to vocal expression and following punctuation when reading aloud. Teachers should instruct students to read at a volume that is quiet without being a whisper. When all groups in a class read this way, it creates a "white noise" effect supporting individual student concentration. When using recordings, the teachers should provide headphones or have the students keep the volume reasonable. Teachers can evaluate student progress by analyzing unpracticed daily readings. While practiced readings will be faster, teachers should stress student improvement over time in unpracticed reading speeds. Experts advise teachers to make use of students they have assigned as "Fluency Leaders" of each small group for collecting and distributing materials and asking questions of the teacher on behalf of their group.

Teachers can differentiate their reading fluency instruction by dividing students into small groups with similar reading levels and fluency rates according to the results of reading and fluency assessments they have made of each student. Teachers can integrate instruction in reading comprehension with instruction in reading fluency. Because high student scores in reading fluency correlate positively with high student scores in reading comprehension, instruction in the two should naturally go together. Teachers can integrate comprehension and fluency by instructing students in "talking to the text" and author as they are reading to enhance their concentration and their understanding of the text. To model metacognition and interactive reading, teachers should periodically conduct a "Think-Aloud" with students, having them verbalize their thoughts about the text to model how students should think about text as they read, and have them practice Think-Alouds in pairs. Teachers can also instruct students in comprehension questions to help them read independently. They can integrate vocabulary development by having students write sentences with context clues for pre-taught vocabulary words.

Example of an item on a formal standards-based reading assessment and how a teacher can interpret this to inform his or her instruction to help the student master English Language Arts standards

On a multiple-choice test, a third-grade student whose family speaks another language is given a picture of a throne and must choose the correct word from choices (A) Thrown, (B) Throne, and (C) Throan. The student selects answer (A) and his answer is marked as incorrect. The student does not understand why his answer choice was marked wrong. From an assessment result such as this, the teacher can determine that this ESL student is having difficulty in distinguishing among homophones—words that sound the same but are spelled differently. This prevents the teacher from assuming that the student's problem is with the correct spelling of English words, or with insufficient knowledge of English vocabulary words. ESL students often make this kind of error: they are likely to see the word *thrown* in print more than *throne*. The teacher can conclude more individualized instruction is indicated to help this student. The teacher should also give the student opportunities to practice telling apart words that sound the same.

Interpreting assessment results to plan instruction in study and research skills

Once teachers have identified student needs in areas like study and research skills, they can plan their instruction accordingly to show students how to use various reference sources and materials, organize information, and relate the information they find to texts and tests in the respective subject content areas. Teacher curriculum planning should include components like the skills and behaviors they will model for students; the direct instruction strategies they will use; the resources, materials, and technology they will utilize; how they will schedule curriculum and instructional activities; and which activities they engage students in for learning. Modeling by teachers and guided practice they will give students should support the direct instruction they deliver to students. They should give students practice in finding and using information from various sources like the Internet, reference books, and other texts; and in remembering and applying information for taking tests.

Areas wherein teachers should assess and instruct students related to comprehension and analysis of literary and narrative texts

Students need to recognize the essential features of important literary genres. These include multicultural literature; poetry, like couplets, lyrics, ballads, epics, and sonnets; drama such as plays; prose, like myths, biographies and autobiographies; and historical and realistic fiction, novels, short stories, legends, and fantasies. Students must also recognize story grammar components like settings, plots, themes, and characters; and additional important aspects of literary texts like point of view, tone, voice, and mood. They must additionally be able to respond to literary narratives and analyze them. Teachers should assess how much students know about these areas, identifying their instructional needs. Teachers should then apply explicit, systematic, research-based instructional strategies to teach students to evaluate the relevance of literary settings; identify recurrent literary themes; recognize the structural components of literary plots and evaluate their credibility and logic; compare and contrast literary characters' motivations and responses; and recognize style elements like figurative language, including metaphors, similes, personification, and hyperbole and literary devices like foreshadowing, imagery, irony, and symbolism.

Assessing a student's reading comprehension in content areas

To assess a student's reading comprehension in content areas, a teacher could use formal tests taken from the text that the student has read, formal tests that the teacher has designed, or informal assessments based on the teacher's observations and discussions of the student's reading. The teacher should assess and instruct the student in recognizing and comprehending different kinds of texts, including expository text, narrative text, and poetic text, and their respective structures. The teacher should also assess and instruct the student in various purposes for reading. Additionally, the teacher should give the student explicit instruction in commonly used text structures, such as cause and effect, comparison and contrast, and so on. The teacher can model for and instruct the student in reading strategies to address different purposes of reading; for example, strategies like scanning, skimming, and reading in depth. The teacher should explicitly instruct the student in study skills for finding and accessing information from content-area texts and reference sources, and for remembering and retrieving information when taking tests.

Applying assessment results to differentiating instruction in reading comprehension

Teachers should assess essential learning content, skills and strategies that students with disabilities or reading problems need and re-teach the background knowledge and linguistic structures and content-area vocabulary that students lack. They should explain tasks and concepts using concrete examples, and ensure extra practice in needed strategies and skills. They can afford students access to grade-level texts by reading them aloud and then leading student discussion. They should help build essential vocabulary, background knowledge, and concepts in content areas for special-needs students, also explaining new activities and concepts using varied concrete examples. They should use multisensory methods engaging vision, hearing, touch, and movement to teach new vocabulary and concepts. These students also benefit from teachers' presenting text orally followed by class or group discussion, and extra practice using informational texts at student levels. Teachers should use scaffolding and explicit modeling strategies with ELL students. They can increase their instructional complexity and/or rates with advanced students, use multiple and/or higher-level texts, increase assignments' breadth and depth, and extend and build upon their existing abilities, knowledge and skills.

Applying student assessment results in oral language and writing for comprehension and analysis of literary or narrative text and literary criticism

Teachers can use a variety of formal and informal assessments to determine what students do or do not know and understand about literary or narrative texts, and skills they do or do not have in literary criticism and narrative text analysis. To address learning needs in these areas, teachers can engage students in explicit oral language activities like Questioning the Author; literature circles for student reading, analysis and discussion; and think-pair-share activities to reinforce and develop existing student skills and teach new ones. Teachers can use explicit writing activities with students like writing summaries of literary texts, writing analyses of literary or narrative characters, and keeping written literary response journals. In all activities, teachers must ensure universal access: when assessing students' background knowledge and existing skills, and when instructing students to develop their skills for understanding and analyzing literary and narrative texts and for literary response, teachers must meet the needs of the entire range of students in their classes. Teachers can apply student assessment data to plan their modeling, direct instruction, and both guided and independent student practice.

Assessing students' development of academic language

In order to develop and use academic language successfully, students must understand the phonological features of the language, have lexical knowledge in the language, have grammatical competence, understand and use discourse, and employ cognition. Discourse involves language units longer a sentence, such as paragraphs. It aids in coherently communicating meaning across multiple sentences, and affords organization in speaking and writing. Discourse can have multiple functions across various communication modalities. For example, it includes using appropriate greetings and pause markers in spoken conversations; using appropriate introductions, transitions, and conclusions, as well as logic, cohesion, and unity when writing; and is able to identify such written elements, including being able to follow logical trains of thought in a text, as well as understanding the relations among paragraphs, chapters, or other segments of a text and developing perspective about the text when reading.

Developing and using academic language consists of knowing, understanding, and applying its component features, including the phonological features of language, the lexical features of language, and grammatical competence in the language, discourse, and cognition. The first five of these features reflect linguistic aspects of academic language. While these are crucially important, cognition is equally vital. Cognition is the act of thinking. When students read, write, and speak, they must think actively about the language and use cognitive processing to understand what they read and hear and to produce accurate, meaningful, expressive written and spoken communications. Some functions wherein student cognition plays an especially vital role include being able to think about a text they read and interpret the meaning the author intended to convey; to infer implied meanings in the text, synthesize meanings in multiple related ideas/sentences/paragraphs/chapters, and predict further events in text before reading them; to read with intention, i.e., for specified purposes, extract factual information from text, and question information sources presented in text.

Learning objective for a lesson in one component of literary analysis

Most educators agree that differentiating and individualizing instruction are beneficial because they can help to erase the achievement gap among students and ensure that all learners succeed. Educators also agree that the main challenge of differentiation is not why but how to do it: they can find it daunting to achieve in actual classroom practice. In teaching literary analysis for comprehension of narrative text, for example, one of many components is character analysis. An example of a learning objective for this is for students to be able to analyze a character in a literary work through identifying a specific character trait, and to supply supporting evidence of their analysis. This can be taught using any work of fiction or nonfiction biography. Cognitive challenges for upper-elementary school students in doing this are using the upper levels of Bloom's taxonomy of cognitive skills, i.e., analysis, synthesis, and evaluation. Educators find that applying these skills is difficult for many of their students.

Learning objective and lesson in one feature of literary analysis

A teacher might design a lesson for a learning objective to identify one character trait in a selected literary or biographical character, and use supporting evidence from text to prove the character personifies that trait. In pre-assessing class skill levels, the teacher might find some students cannot do any of these, others who can identify a trait but cannot locate supporting evidence or write the analysis, and others can identify a trait and locate supporting evidence but need practice writing the response. To differentiate instruction for these three groups, teachers will have to do the following: (1) Supply students the character and trait. Students write on Post-it notes three pieces of supporting evidence, and why each piece proves the character embodies the trait. (2) Supply a character and list of traits and students choose one trait, using Post-it notes like the first group to construct responses. (3) Assign character and trait selection to students. Students find three pieces of supporting evidence, using Post-it notes (or not) as needed. Students write responses using their notes of evidence.

Teaching story structure

Children's natural interest in stories provides a perfect occasion for teaching them about the structure of narrative text. When teachers read a story aloud to students in the early elementary grades, or give them a reading lesson, they can use these as opportunities to identify narrative structure. This affords a framework for students to talk about and retell a story. For example, when reading a story, the teacher can ask the students the following: What is the title of this story? Who is the main character in the story? What happened first? What happened next? What happened at the end of the story? Where does this story take place? And what is the theme or point of this story? Teachers and students can discuss these structural elements. Also, when teachers consistently target the same story elements for identifying the key features in a story, this offers the students recurring opportunities for discussing story structure and making connections among texts about their sequences and main characters.

One specific student skill as a component of literary analysis and an example of an associated lesson objective

Literary analysis includes various components like settings, themes, plots, and characters, among others. For the component of character analysis, teachers might designate a learning objective for third- to fifth-graders of identifying a particular character trait, explaining how the character demonstrates that trait, and supplying specific evidence to support their explanation. Before teaching the lesson, as for any differentiated instruction, teachers should conduct a pre-assessment to determine their various students' degrees of development in this skill. For example, a teacher might discover from the results of such an assessment that the students could be grouped into three general skill levels. One group is not able to identify a suitable character trait, cannot locate any supportive evidence, and does not know how to write an appropriate response to meet the lesson objective. A second group can identify a character trait, but cannot find any evidence to support it or write a response. A third group is able to identify a fitting character trait and locate evidence in the text, but needs practice in writing an appropriate response.

Hypothetical scenario for an objective and lesson in literary character analysis

To teach character analysis to upper-elementary students, a teacher might use a lesson objective in which students select a literary character, identify one character trait, and use supporting text evidence to explain how the character manifests that trait. Teachers can differentiate instruction by supplying character and trait for students who cannot do any of these, having them write pieces of evidence on Post-it notes for writing. For students who can select characters but not do the other parts, teachers supply a character, have students choose a trait from a provided list, and use Post-its like the first group. For students who can select characters, traits, and evidence, teachers can have them make their own selections and practice writing. This assignment can be printed on paper strips that students paste into journals. Student advantages include graduated complexity levels and privacy regarding individualization. Teachers find this lesson highly manageable. Considerations include continual reassessment to monitor progress, and not "tracking" students into groups without "graduating" them to successive levels when indicated.

Relationship of mental constructs to processes in reading

Some researchers believe that because readers' schemata affect their metacognitive processes and the inferences they make, schemata can also vary in the information that is available, the automaticity of the inferences that the readers make, and the kinds of monitoring strategies that the readers apply. Because narrative is considered to demand more global processing and exposition requires more local processing, readers will construct better integrated and broader schemes of narrative texts: they will take different information from them, and they will be able to answer different kinds of standardized test questions about them. Reading curricula frequently exploit the more global character of narrative texts in teaching students to make story maps and/or concept maps by applying pre-established structures, as defined by certain types of story grammars; and using dramatic arcs and temporal sequencing for instructing students in reading narratives. Moreover, readers find it easier to remember texts that have familiar structures, which are more likely with narrative texts than expository texts.

Supporting student comprehension of informational and expository texts

To help students understand informational or expository texts, teachers can instruct students explicitly to evaluate the structural patterns, logic, internal consistency, unity of the point of view, perspective, and/or argument set forth by the authors of these texts; to analyze how an author developed his or her perspective, point of view, and/or argument; to identify the differences and similarities among various informational texts; and to generalize what they learn from expository texts to other learning areas. To teach students how to find meaning in expository texts in different ways, teachers can directly instruct students in strategies to read these texts for various purposes. Teachers can instruct students in reading skills like browsing, previewing, skimming, and reading in depth. Teachers should model these strategies and skills for students, and provide them with guided practice activities to gain experience in using them to obtain meaning from informational texts. Teachers should also ensure that students apply these reading strategies across the content areas of the curriculum.

Research into elementary students' reading comprehension of narrative versus expository text

Extant psycholinguistic research indicates that reading expository texts requires local processing, whereas narrative text requires both local and global processing. Some educational researchers have found different student reading performances partly attributable to structural differences between these genres. Researchers controlled for text difficulty and content in tasks involving reading narrative and exposition. When they used a "Think-Along Passage" (TAP), wherein students answered questions after each page during reading—which required local processing only—students showed no differences between genres. But when students had to retell the whole text after reading—a task which required global processing—they recalled narrative better than exposition. These results agreed with psycholinguistic findings. Researchers conclude it can be instructionally more effective to focus on key differences and similarities between genres than simple exposure to or instruction about narrative and exposition. Differences prevent students from approaching both genres the same way, while similarities improve transfer and generalization. Additionally, other researchers found most middle-grades social studies texts to be poor examples of exposition, causing more problems for struggling readers than good ones.

Recent issues in reading assessment

Educators find that high-stakes standardized tests still define reading comprehension, but such test formats are limited and are designed for group administration, quick scoring, and minimal teacher interpretation. Also, assessment sensitivity varies by student age, motivation, and skill; and by test format, items, and text difficulty. Reading comprehension for elementary school students is given lower priority before the third grade. Moreover, assessments are very limited for ESL students, struggling readers, and even more limited for non-readers. Variety among text genres is limited on the formal tests available. Formal reading evaluations often have little or no connection to disciplinary knowledge and thinking. Assessment results usually reflect one-time "snapshots" of performance, not accurately applicable to longer-term learning and gradual progress and not reflecting all aspects of student reading comprehension skills. In addition, very few performance measures exist of verbal synthesis, critiquing, debate, and discussion.

Informal assessments of reading comprehension with elementary school students

Teachers usually assess the reading comprehension of elementary grade students using observation, anecdotal records, student answers to questions about text, having students retell text they read, having students write responses to text they read, and holding reading discussion groups. Critics say informal reading assessments are not aligned with any standards, are not uniform in nature, are not quantitative, and are too subjective. They find that, to measure growth, demonstrate achievement, and compare schools, hard data are required rather than informal assessment results. Informal reading inventories may include measures of oral reading accuracy, ratings of fluency reading aloud, reading rates measures, retelling reading content, comprehension questions, and graded word lists. Of these, educators should collect data for students in grades K-3 on their reading rates, oral reading accuracy, fluency ratings, their answers to reading comprehension questions, and their ability to retell reading content.

Information sources from which teachers need to obtain assessment data

Teachers need to collect data from multiple reading passages on multiple grade and skill levels. They must gather information about student reading of multiple text genres, using multiple word lists, and from silent reading by students reading above third-grade level. The reasons for silent reading data are because reading comprehension and reading accuracy are unrelated for many students, reading silently lets students look back at what they have read and apply different or additional strategies to correct or improve comprehension, and reading silently prevents the performance-affecting social anxiety many students experience when reading aloud. Informal reading inventories (IRIs) are diagnostic if teachers interpret miscues, self-corrections, and oral reading patterns; identify problems with retelling and/or answering specific questions; use findings in parent and student conferences; and align reading instruction and materials with student needs. IRIs are effective if teachers are well-trained; IRIs are used schoolwide and/or district-wide; administrators and parents value IRIs; and educators use technology (e.g., handheld devices like tablets or smartphones) to collect data.

Planning literacy-rich environments

The three design principles for creating literacy-rich environments are definition, adaptation, and familiarity. The principle of definition entails clearly delineating play areas. For example, teachers can add environmental print by labeling each learning center and posting directional signs, materials inventories, and ideas or suggestions for material use, like signs or posters in an "office" area saying "Sign-in sheet," "Dial 911 for emergencies," "Phone messages," and "Remember to recycle." The principle of adaptation entails modifying typical areas to approximate real-life literacy settings. For example, a play kitchen can become a restaurant by adding real-life reading and writing activity props (e.g., a restaurant sign, a "Shoes and Shirt Required" sign, a "Daily Specials" chalkboard, menus, order-taking pads, and magazine and newspaper racks). The principle of familiarity entails inserting literacy objects into familiar settings. For example, in a classroom's building-block area, teachers can add blueprints, order forms, invoices, and children's books about construction projects. Teachers can also encourage children's designing and making complex, long-term projects using multiple symbolic languages and literacy dimensions and media such as words and gestures to drawing and writing, to diagrams, to blocks and manipulatives, to three-dimensional models, to paintings and 3-D collages, drama, dance, and so forth.

Practice Test

Practice Questions

1. *Sea* and *see*, *fair* and *fare*, are called:
    a. Homophones
    b. Antonyms
    c. Homographs
    d. Twin words

2. Another name for a persuasive essay is:
    a. Dynamic essay
    b. Convincing essay
    c. Argumentative essay
    d. Position paper

3. A teacher is working with a group of third graders at the same reading level. Her goal is to improve reading fluency. She asks each child in turn to read a page from a book about mammal young. She asks the children to read with expression. She also reminds them they don't need to stop between each word; they should read as quickly as they comfortably can. She cautions them, however, not to read so quickly that they leave out or misread a word. The teacher knows the components of reading fluency are:
    a. Speed, drama, and comprehension
    b. Cohesion, rate, and prosody
    c. Understanding, rate, and prosody
    d. Rate, accuracy, and prosody

4. "Language load" refers to:
    a. The basic vocabulary words a first grader has committed to memory
    b. The number of unrecognizable words an English Language Learner encounters when reading a passage or listening to a teacher
    c. The damage that carrying a pile of heavy books could cause to a child's physique
    d. The number of different languages a person has mastered.

5. A syllable must contain:
    a. A vowel
    b. A consonant
    c. Both a vowel and a consonant
    d. A meaning

6. A third-grade teacher has several students reading above grade level. Most of the remaining students are reading at grade level. There are also a few students reading below grade level. She decides to experiment. Her hypothesis is that by giving the entire class a chapter book above grade level, high-level readers will be satisfied, grade-level readers will be challenged in a positive way, and students reading below grade level will be inspired to improve. Her method is most likely to:

    a. Succeed, producing students reading at an Instructional reading level. High-level readers will be happy to be given material appropriate to their reading level. Grade-level readers will challenge themselves to improve reading strategies in order to master the text. Because only a few of the students are reading below grade level, the other students, who feel happy and energized, will inspire the slower readers by modeling success.

    b. Succeed, producing students reading at an Independent reading level. High-level readers will independently help grade-level readers who will, in turn, independently help those below grade level.

    c. Fail, producing students at a Frustration reading level. Those reading below grade level are likely to give up entirely. Those reading at grade level are likely to get frustrated and form habits that will actually slow down their development.

    d. Fail, producing students reading at a Chaotic reading level. By nature, children are highly competitive. The teacher has not taken into consideration multiple learning styles. The children who are at grade level will either become bitter and angry at those whose reading level is above grade level or simply give up. The children reading below grade level will not be able to keep up and will in all likelihood act out their frustration or completely shut down.

7. Of the three tiers of words, the most important words for direct instruction are:

    a. Tier-one words

    b. Common words

    c. Tier-two words

    d. Words with Latin roots

8. At the beginning of each month, Mr. Yi has Jade read a page or two from a book she hasn't seen before. He notes the total number of words in the section, and also notes the number of times she leaves out or misreads a word. If Jade reads the passage with less than 3% error, Mr. Yi is satisfied that Jade is:

    a. Reading with full comprehension

    b. Probably bored and should try a more difficult book

    c. Reading at her Independent reading level

    d. Comfortable with the syntactical meaning

9. The purpose of corrective feedback is:

    a. To provide students with methods for explaining to the teacher or classmates what a passage was about

    b. To correct an error in reading a student has made, specifically clarifying where and how the error was made so that the student can avoid similar errors in the future

    c. To provide a mental framework that will help the student correctly organize new information

    d. To remind students that error is essential in order to truly understand and that it is not something to be ashamed of

10. Dr. Jenks is working with a group of high school students. They are about to read a science book about fossils. Before they begin, she writes the words *stromatolites, fossiliferous,* and *eocene* on the board. She explains the meaning of each word. These words are examples of:
   a. Academic words
   b. Alliteration
   c. Content-specific words
   d. Ionization

11. Which of the following best explains the importance prior knowledge brings to the act of reading?
   a. Prior knowledge is information the student gets through researching a topic prior to reading the text. A student who is well-prepared through such research is better able to decode a text and retain its meaning.
   b. Prior knowledge is knowledge the student brings from previous life or learning experiences to the act of reading. It is not possible for a student to fully comprehend new knowledge without first integrating it with prior knowledge.
   c. Prior knowledge is predictive. It motivates the student to look for contextual clues in the reading and predict what is likely to happen next.
   d. Prior knowledge is not important to any degree to the act of reading, because every text is self-contained and therefore seamless. Prior knowledge is irrelevant in this application.

12. A cloze test evaluates a student's:
   a. Reading fluency
   b. Understanding of context and vocabulary
   c. Phonemic skills
   d. Ability to apply the alphabetic principle to previously unknown material

13. Sight words are:
   a. Common words with irregular spelling
   b. Words that can easily be found on educational websites
   c. Any word that can be seen, including text words, words on signs, brochures, banners, and so forth
   d. There is no such thing; because oral language is learned before written language, all words are ultimately based on sound. The correct term is sound words and includes all words necessary to decode a particular text

14. *Ph*one, *th*ey, *ch*urch. The underlined letters in these words are examples of:
   a. Consonant blend
   b. Consonant shift
   c. Continental shift
   d. Consonant digraph

15. Phonemic awareness is a type of:
   a. Phonological awareness. Phonemic awareness is the ability to recognize sounds within words
   b. Phonics. It is a teaching technique whereby readers learn the relationship between letters and sounds
   c. Alphabetization. Unless a reader knows the alphabet, phonemic awareness is useless
   d. Syntactical awareness. Understanding the underlying structure of a sentence is key to understanding meaning

16. All members of a group of kindergarten students early in the year are able to chant the alphabet. The teacher is now teaching the students what the alphabet looks like in written form. The teacher points to a letter and the students vocalize the correspondent sound. Alternatively, the teacher vocalizes a phoneme and a student points to it on the alphabet chart. The teacher is using _____ in her instruction.
   a. Letter–sound correspondence
   b. Rote memorization
   c. Predictive analysis
   d. Segmentation

17. A fourth-grade teacher is preparing her students for a reading test in which a number of words have been replaced with blanks. The test will be multiple-choice; there are three possible answers given for each blank. The teacher instructs the children to read all the possible answers and cross out any answer that obviously doesn't fit. Next, the students should "plug in" the remaining choices and eliminate any that are grammatically incorrect or illogical. Finally, the student should consider contextual clues in order to select the best answer. This in an example of:
   a. Strategy instruction
   b. Diagnostic instruction
   c. Skills instruction
   d. Multiple-choice instruction

18. The term "common words" means:
   a. One-syllable words with fewer than three letters. Some examples are it, an, a, I, go, to, and in. They are the first words an emergent writer learns
   b. One-syllable words with fewer than five letters. Some examples include sing, goes, sit, rock, walk, and took
   c. Words that are ordinary or unexceptional; because they tend to flatten a piece of writing, they should be avoided
   d. Familiar, frequently used words that do not need to be taught beyond primary grades

19. Which is greater, the number of English phonemes or the number of letters in the alphabet?
   a. The number of letters in the alphabet, because they can be combined to create phonemes
   b. The number of phonemes. A phoneme is the smallest measure of language sound
   c. They are identical; each letter "owns" a correspondent sound
   d. Neither. Phonemes and alphabet letters are completely unrelated

20. *Train, brain, spring.* The underlined letters are examples of:
  a. Consonant digraph
  b. Consonant blend
  c. Consonant shift
  d. Continental shift

21. It is the beginning of the school year. To determine which second-grade students might need support, the reading teacher wants to identify those who are reading below grade level. She works with students one at a time. She gives each child a book at a second-grade reading level and asks the child to read out loud for two minutes. Children who will need reading support are those who read:
  a. Fewer than 100 words in the time given
  b. Fewer than 200 words in the time given
  c. More than 75 words in the time given
  d. The entire book in the time given

22. The most effective strategy for decoding sight words is:
  a. Segmenting sight words into syllables. Beginning readers are understandably nervous when encountering a long word that isn't familiar. Blocking off all but a single syllable at a time renders a word manageable and allows the reader a sense of control over the act of reading
  b. Word families. By grouping the sight word with similar words, patterns emerge
  c. A phonemic approach. When students understand the connection between individual words and their sounds, they will be able to sound out any sight word they encounter
  d. None; sight words cannot be decoded. Readers must learn to recognize these words as wholes on sight

23. Which of the following choices will be most important when designing a reading activity or lesson for students?
  a. Selecting a text
  b. Determining the number of students participating
  c. Analyzing the point in the school year at which the lesson is given
  d. Determining a purpose for instruction

24. "Decoding" is also called:
  a. Remediation
  b. Deciphering
  c. Alphabetic principle
  d. Deconstruction

25. Which text(s) are likely to foster the greatest enthusiasm for reading and literature among students?
  a. Free choice of reading texts, provided that students complete class assignments, projects, and discussions
  b. An all-in-one textbook that includes all reading material for the year, study guides, and sample test questions
  c. A variety of texts, including books, magazines, newspapers, stories from oral traditions, poetry, music, and films
  d. A small selection of current best-selling books for children, some of which the children may already have read and liked

26. Phonological awareness activities are:
   a. Oral
   b. Visual
   c. Both A and B
   d. Semantically based

27. A student is able to apply strategies to comprehend the meanings of unfamiliar words; can supply definitions for words with several meanings such as *crucial, criticism,* and *witness*; and is able to reflect on her background knowledge in order to decipher a word's meaning. These features of effective reading belong to which category?
   a. Word recognition
   b. Vocabulary
   c. Content
   d. Comprehension

28. A reading teacher is assessing an eighth grader to determine her reading level. Timed at a minute, the student reads with 93% accuracy. She misreads an average of seven words out of 100. What is her reading level?
   a. She is reading at a Frustration level
   b. She is reading at an Excellence level
   c. She is reading at an Instructional level
   d. She is reading at an Independent level

29. When should students learn how to decode?
   a. Decoding is the most basic and essential strategy to becoming a successful reader. It should be introduced to kindergartners during the first two weeks of school
   b. Decoding is not a teachable skill. It is an unconscious act and is natural to all learners
   c. Decoding should be taught only after children have mastered every letter–sound relationship as well as every consonant digraph and consonant blend. They should also be able to recognize and say the 40 phonemes common to English words and be able to recognize at least a dozen of the most common sight words
   d. Decoding depends on an understanding of letter–sound relationships. As soon as a child understands enough letters and their correspondent sounds to read a few words, decoding should be introduced

30. *Since, whether,* and *accordingly* are examples of which type of signal words?
   a. Common, or basic, signal words
   b. Compare/contrast words
   c. Cause–effect words
   d. Temporal sequencing words

31. A class is reading *The Heart Is a Lonely Hunter*. The teacher asks students to write a short paper explaining the story's resolution. She is asking them to locate and discuss the story's:
   a. Outcome
   b. Highest or most dramatic moment
   c. Plot
   d. Lowest point

32. A student encounters a multisyllabic word. She's not sure if she's seen it before. What should she do first? What should she do next?
   a. Locate familiar word parts, then locate the consonants
   b. Locate the consonants, then locate the vowels
   c. Locate the vowels, then locate familiar word parts
   d. Look it up in the dictionary, then write down the meaning

The following passage pertains to the following questions 33 - 36:

The kindergarten teacher is concerned about three of her students. While they are enthusiastic about writing, they do not always recognize letters, confusing b, d, and p, or e and o. They do, however, know which sounds go with certain letters when they are orally drilled. When they write, they appear to be attempting letter–sound associations.

"Now I'm writing *M*," the teacher heard one boy say as he scripted a large *N* in the upper right corner of his paper. He studied it for a moment and added, "Nope, it needs another leg." The student then wrote an *I* beside the *N*. "There," he said. "Now you are an *M*. I can write the word, 'man,' because now I have *M*." The child then moved to the lower left corner of the paper. "M-A-N," he said to himself, slowly pronouncing each sound. "I already have that *M*. Here is where the rest of the word goes." He turned the paper sideways and wrote *N*.

The second child sang to herself as she gripped the crayon and scribbled lines here and there on her paper. Some of the lines resembled letters, but few actually were. Others were scribbles. As she "wrote," she seemed to be making up a story and seemed to believe she was writing the story down.

The third child didn't vocalize at all while he worked. He gripped the paper and carefully wrote the same letter over and over and over. Sometimes the letter was large, sometimes tiny. He turned the paper in every direction so that sometimes the letter was sideways or upside down. Sometimes he flipped it backward. "What are you writing?" the teacher asked him. "My name," the child told her. The teacher then realized the letter was, indeed, the first letter of his name. She gently told him he had done a fine job of writing the first letter of his name. Did he want her to help him write the rest of it? "Nope," he cheerfully told her, "it's all here." He pointed at one of the letters and "read" his full name. He pointed at another letter and again seemed to believe it represented all the sounds of his name.

33. The kindergarten teacher isn't certain if these children are exhibiting signs of a reading disability or other special needs. What should the teacher do?
   a. Nothing. These children are simply at an early stage in the reading/writing process
   b. Nothing. She doesn't want to have to tell the parents that their children are sub-par in terms of intelligence. They are perfectly nice children and can contribute to society in other ways. She resolves to give them extra attention in other areas to help them build confidence
   c. She should recommend that the parents take the children to be tested for a number of reading disorders, including dyslexia
   d. She should arrange a meeting between herself, the school psychologist, and the reading specialist to discuss the matter and resolve it using a three-pronged approach

34. In the above example, the emergent writers are demonstrating their understanding that letters symbolize predictable sounds, that words begin with an initial sound/letter, and that by "writing," they are empowering themselves by offering a reader access to their thoughts and ideas. The next three stages the emergent writers will pass through in order will most likely be:
    a. Scripting the end-sound to a word (KT=cat); leaving space between words; writing from the top left to the top right of the page, and from top to bottom
    b. Scripting the end-sound to a word (KT=cat); writing from the top left to the top right of the page, and from top to bottom; separating the words from one another with a space between
    c. Leaving space between the initial letters that represent words; writing from the top left to the top right of the page, and from top to bottom; scripting the final sound of each word as well as the initial sound (KT=cat)
    d. Drawing a picture beside each of the initial sounds to represent the entire word; scripting the end-sound to a word (KT=cat); scripting the interior sounds that compose the entire word (KAT=cat)

35. The teacher might best encourage the three students in the above example by:
    a. Suggesting they write an entire book rather than just a single page. This will build confidence, teach them sequencing, and encourage the young writers to delve deeper into their ideas.
    b. Ask the students to read their stories to her. Suggest they visit other children in the class and read to each of them.
    c. Contact the local newspaper and invite a reporter to visit her class and write a story about her emergent writers. In this way, they are sure to see themselves as "real writers" and will more fully apply themselves to the task.
    d. Invite all the parents to visit the class the following week. This will give all classmates, regardless of where they are on the learning spectrum, time to memorize their stories. The children will be very excited and will begin to see themselves as "real writers."

36. At what point should the kindergarten teacher in the above example offer the three children picture books and ask them to read to her?
    a. When the three children are all able to script initial sounds, end sounds, and interior sounds they are ready to decode words. She should make her request at this point
    b. As each child reaches the stage in which he or she can script initial sounds, end sounds, and interior sounds, the teacher should ask only that child to read to her
    c. As each child reaches the stage in which he habitually writes from the top to the bottom of the page, moving left to right, the time has come. Books are intended to be read in this way, and until a child has had the experience of writing in the same manner, he won't be able to make sense of the words
    d. The teacher should encourage all students to "read" picture books from the first day of school. Talking about the pictures from page to page gives young readers the idea that books are arranged sequentially. Pictures also offer narrative coherence and contextual clues. Emergent readers who are encouraged to enjoy books will more readily embrace the act of reading. Holding a book and turning pages gives young readers a familiarity with them

37. Which of the following statements regarding the acquisition of language is false?
   a. Young children often have the ability to comprehend written language just as early as they can comprehend or reproduce oral language when given appropriate instruction
   b. Oral language typically develops before a child understands the relationship between spoken and written word
   c. Most young children are first exposed to written language when an adult reads aloud
   d. A child's ability to speak, read, and write depends on a variety of physiological factors, as well as environmental factors

38. A teacher is teaching students analogizing. She is teaching them to:
   a. Identify and use metaphors
   b. Identify and use similes
   c. Identify and use groups of letters that occur in a word family
   d. Identify and use figures of speech

39. A reading teacher is working with a student who has just moved to Texas from Korea. The child knows very few words in English. The teacher offers her a picture book of Korean folk tales. Using words and gestures, the teacher asks her to "read" one folk tale. The child "reads" the familiar tale in Korean. The teacher then writes key English words on the board and asks the child to find those words in the book. When the child finds the words, they read them together. This strategy is:
   a. Useful. The child will feel more confident because the story is already familiar. She will also feel that the lesson is a conversation of sorts, and that she is communicating successfully. She will be motivated to learn the English words because they are meaningful and highly charged
   b. Useful. The teacher is learning as much as the child is. The teacher is learning about Korean culture and language, and she can apply this knowledge when teaching future Korean students
   c. Not very useful. The child needs to be exposed to as much American culture as possible. Encouraging her to remember her own culture will make her sad and will limit her curiosity about her new home
   d. Not very useful. The first things the child should learn are the letters of the alphabet and associative sounds. Only then can she begin to decipher an unfamiliar language

40. The teacher in the previous question was using what kind of load?
   a. Language load
   b. Cognitive load
   c. Bilingual load
   d. Cultural load

41. Using brain imaging, researchers have discovered that dyslexic readers use the _____ side(s) of their brains, while non-dyslexic readers use the _____ side(s) of their brains.
   a. Left; right
   b. Right; left
   c. Right and left; left
   d. Right; left and right

42. A fifth grader has prepared a report on reptiles, which is something he knows a great deal about. He rereads his report and decides to make a number of changes. He moves a sentence from the top to the last paragraph. He crosses out several words and replaces them with more specific words. He circles key information and draws an arrow to show another place the information could logically be placed. He is engaged in:
   a. Editing
   b. Revising
   c. First editing, then revising
   d. Reviewing

43. *Bi, re,* and *un* are:
   a. Suffixes, appearing at the beginning of base words to change their meaning
   b. Suffixes, appearing at the end of base words to enhance their meaning
   c. Prefixes, appearing at the beginning of base words to emphasize their meaning
   d. Prefixes, appearing at the beginning of base words to change their meanings

44. Examples of CVC words include:
   a. Add, pad, mad
   b. Cat, tack, act
   c. Elephant, piano, examine
   d. Dog, sit, leg

45. A teacher is working with a student who is struggling with reading. The teacher gives him a story with key words missing:

> The boy wanted to take the dog for a walk. The boy opened the door. The _____ ran out. The ___ looked for the dog. When he found the dog, he was very _____.

The student is able to fill in the blanks by considering:
   a. Syntax. Oftentimes, word order gives enough clues that a reader can predict what happens next.
   b. Pretext. By previewing the story, the student can deduce the missing words.
   c. Context. By considering the other words in the story, the student can determine the missing words.
   d. Sequencing. By putting the ideas in logical order, the student can determine the missing words.

46. The following is/are (an) element(s) of metacognition:
   a. A reader's awareness of herself as a learner
   b. A reader's understanding of a variety of reading strategies and how to apply them to comprehend a text
   c. A reader who is conscious about remembering what has been read
   d. All of the above

47. Collaborative Strategic Reading (CSR) is a teaching technique that depends on two teaching practices. These practices are:
   a. Cooperative learning and reading comprehension
   b. Cooperative reading and metacognition
   c. Reading comprehension and metacognition
   d. Cooperative learning and metacognition

48. Context clues are useful in:
   a. Predicting future action
   b. Understanding the meaning of words that are not familiar
   c. Understanding character motivation
   d. Reflecting on a text's theme

49. A teacher has a child who does not volunteer in class. When the teacher asks the student a question the student can answer, she does so with as few words as possible. The teacher isn't sure how to best help the child. She should:
   a. Leave the child alone. She is clearly very shy and will be embarrassed by having attention drawn to her. She is learning in her own way.
   b. Ask two or three highly social children to include this girl in their activities. She is shy, and she probably won't approach them on her own.
   c. Observe the child over the course of a week or two. Draw her into conversation and determine if her vocabulary is limited, if she displays emotional problems, or if her reticence could have another cause. Note how the child interacts with others in the class. Does she ever initiate conversation? If another child initiates, does she respond?
   d. Refer her to the school counselor immediately. It is clear the child is suffering from either a low IQ or serious problems at home.

50. For their monthly project, a group of students can choose to read and respond to one book on a list supplied by their teacher. The books are grouped according to genre. Most students choose books listed under the genre that is described as "modern-day stories that are not true, but seem as though they could really happen." Which genre did most of the students choose from?
   a. Historical fiction
   b. Autobiography
   c. Realistic fiction
   d. Fantasy

51. A high school class reads an essay about the possible effects of sexual activity on teens. The author's position is very clear: She believes young people should avoid sex because they aren't mature enough to take the necessary steps to remain safe. The author cites facts, research studies, and statistics to strengthen her position. This type of writing is called:
   a. Expository
   b. Narrative
   c. Persuasive
   d. Didactic

52. A reading teacher feels that some of his strategies aren't effective. He has asked a specialist to observe him and make suggestions as to how he can improve. The reading specialist should suggest that first:
 a. The teacher set up a video camera and record several sessions with different students for the specialist to review. The presence of an observer changes the outcome; if the specialist is in the room, it will negatively affect the students' ability to read
 b. The teacher reflects on his strategies himself. Which seem to work? Which don't? Can the teacher figure out why? It's always best to encourage teachers to find their own solutions so that they can handle future issues themselves
 c. They meet to discuss areas the teacher is most concerned about and decide on the teacher's goals
 d. The specialist should arrive unannounced to observe the teacher interacting with students. This will prevent the teacher from unconsciously over-preparing

53. A kindergarten teacher pronounces a series of word pairs for her students. The students repeat the pairs. Some of the pairs rhyme (*see/bee*) and some of the pairs share initial sounds but do not rhyme (*sit, sun*). The students help her separate the word pairs into pairs that rhyme and pairs that do not. Once the students are able to distinguish between two words that rhyme and two words that do not, the teacher says a word and asks them to provide a rhyme. When she says *cat* a child responds with *fat*. When she says *sing* a child offers *thing*. How does this strictly oral activity contribute to the children's ability to read?
 a. It doesn't. Oral activities must have a written component to be useful to emergent readers
 b. It is helpful in that it demonstrates how different sounds are made with different letters
 c. It actually discourages children from reading. By emphasizing orality over literacy, the teacher is suggesting to the children that reading is not an important skill
 d. Being able to identify rhyme is an important element of phonological awareness

54. Syllable types include:
 a. Closed, open, silent e, vowel team, vowel-r, and consonant-le
 b. Closed, open, silent, double-vowel, r, and le
 c. Closed, midway, open, emphasized, prefixed, and suffixed
 d. Stressed, unstressed, and silent

55. An eighth-grade student is able to decode most words fluently and has a borderline/acceptable vocabulary, but his reading comprehension is quite low. He can be helped with instructional focus on:
 a. Strategies to increase comprehension and to build vocabulary
 b. Strategies to increase comprehension and to be able to identify correct syntactical usage
 c. Strategies to improve his understanding of both content and context
 d. Strategies to build vocabulary and to improve his understanding of both content and context

56. Reading comprehension and vocabulary can best be assessed:
    a. With brief interviews and tests every two months to determine how much learning has taken place. Students learn in spurts, and in-depth assessments of comprehension and vocabulary are a waste of time
    b. Through a combination of standardized testing, informal teacher observations, attention to grades, objective-linked assessments, and systematized charting of data over time
    c. By giving students weekly self-assessment rubrics to keep them constantly aware of and invested in their own progress
    d. By having students retell a story or summarize the content of an informational piece of writing. The degree to which the material was comprehended, and the richness or paucity of vocabulary used in such work, provides efficient and thorough assessment

57. An ORF is:
    a. An Oral Reading Fluency assessment
    b. An Occasional Reading Function assessment
    c. An Oscar Reynolds Feinstein assessment
    d. An Overt Reading Failure assessment

58. Round-robin reading refers to the practice of allowing children to take turns reading portions of a text aloud to the rest of the group during class. Which of the following statements is <u>least</u> true about this practice?
    a. Students have the chance to practice reading aloud with this strategy
    b. This practice is ineffective in its use of time, leaving students who are not reading aloud to become bored or daydream
    c. Round-robin reading lacks the creativity or engaging qualities that will interest students in building literacy skills
    d. This practice helps students feel comfortable with reading aloud due to continuous practice and encouragement from the teacher and peers

59. Word-recognition ability is:
    a. Equally important to all readers
    b. Used only by fluent readers
    c. Another term for "word attack"
    d. Especially important to English Language Learners and students with reading disabilities

60. Research indicates that developing oral language proficiency in emergent readers is important because:
    a. Proficiency with oral language enhances students' phonemic awareness and increases vocabulary
    b. The more verbally expressive emergent readers are, the more confident they become. Such students will embrace both Academic and Independent reading levels
    c. It encourages curiosity about others. With strong oral language skills, students begin to question the world around them. The more they ask, the richer their background knowledge
    d. It demonstrates to students that their ideas are important and worth sharing

61. In preparation for writing a paper, a high school class has been instructed to skim a number of Internet and print documents. They are being asked to:
   a. Read the documents several times, skimming to a deeper level of understanding each time
   b. Read the documents quickly, looking for those that offer the most basic, general information
   c. Read the documents quickly, looking for key words in order to gather the basic premise of each
   d. Read the documents carefully, looking for those that offer the most in-depth information

62. The students in the above question are most likely preparing to write a(n) _____ essay:
   a. Personal
   b. Expository
   c. Literary
   d. Narrative

A teacher has given the first paragraph of an essay to her students to analyze and discuss. Read the paragraph and answer the following questions 63-65:

Americans have struggled with cigarettes far too long. Until now, it has been a personal choice to smoke (or not), but the time for change is rapidly approaching. Local legislation has already begun for schools, restaurants, arenas, and other public places to be smoke-free. Years ago cigarette smoking was presented by the media as being fashionable, even sexy. In magazines, movies, and later in television, celebrities would indulge themselves with a smoke and even be paid to endorse a brand. As recently as 1975, it was common for talk show hosts like Tom Snyder and Johnny Carson to keep a cigarette burning. Cigarette smoking in America has persisted in spite of frightening concerns like lung cancer and emphysema. Over the years, the tobacco industry has sought to diffuse strong evidence that smoking is harmful. However, the myth of "safe cigarettes," questions about nicotine addiction, and denials about the dangers of secondhand smoke have proven to be propaganda and lies.

63. This is a(n) _____ essay:
   a. Compare/contrast
   b. Persuasive
   c. Narrative
   d. Analytic

64. The thesis statement is:
   a. However, the myth of "safe cigarettes," questions about nicotine addiction, and denials about the dangers of secondhand smoke have proven to be propaganda and lies
   b. Americans have struggled with cigarettes far too long
   c. Until now, it has been a personal choice to smoke (or not), but the time for change is rapidly approaching
   d. In magazines, movies, and later in television, celebrities would indulge themselves with a smoke and even be paid to endorse a brand

65. The next three paragraphs in the essay will most likely address:
   a. Smoking as a personal choice, changes in local legislation, and how fashionable smoking once was
   b. How fashionable smoking once was, talk show hosts smoking on air, the myth of "safe cigarettes"
   c. Propaganda and lies, the myth of "safe cigarettes," and how long Americans have struggled with cigarettes
   d. The myth of "safe cigarettes," questions about nicotine addiction, and the dangers of secondhand smoke

66. The teacher and her students brainstorm a list of talents, skills, and specialized knowledge belonging to members of the class. Some of the items on the list include how to make a soufflé, how to juggle, and how to teach a dog to do tricks. One student knows a great deal about spiders, and another about motorcycles. She asks each student to write an essay about something he or she is good at or knows a great deal about. What kind of essay is she asking the students to produce?
   a. Cause and effect
   b. Compare/contrast
   c. Example
   d. Argumentative

67. *Caret, carrot, to, two and too* share something in common. They:
   a. Are nouns
   b. Are monosyllabic
   c. Are homophones
   d. Represent things in nature

Questions 68 – 70 pertain to the following paragraph:

   A class will visit an assisted living facility to interview residents about their lives. Each group of three has selected a theme such as love, work, or personal accomplishment and written several questions around that theme. Next each group practices interviewing one another. The teacher then asks all the students to discuss the questions that caused them to respond most thoughtfully, as well as those they were less inspired by. The students decided the questions that were easiest to respond to asked for very specific information; for example, one inspiring question was, "Please tell me about something you learned to do as a child that affected the direction of your life." Those that were uninspiring were too broad, for example, "Please tell me about your happiest memory."

68. After they interview the residents, each group of three students will work together to write a piece about the resident. This kind of approach is called:
   a. Collaborative learning
   b. Companion learning
   c. Bonded learning
   d. Group learning

69. The genre the teacher expects is:
    a. Memoir
    b. Historical fiction
    c. Biography
    d. Autobiography

70. The teacher wants the students to apply what they've learned across content areas. Which of the following strategies would be most effective?
    a. Students will interview a family member, asking the same questions
    b. Students will write a personal piece in which they address the same questions
    c. Students will do online research about the cultural, economic, or political events that were occurring during the specific time about which they've written
    d. Students pretend to be the interviewee and rewrite the piece from a first person point of view

The following passage pertains to questions 71 – 73:

A seventh-grade teacher asks the reading teacher to suggest a lesson students will find simultaneously challenging and fun. The reading teacher suggests the class read fairy tales from both Hans Christian Anderson and the Brothers Grimm and have a rapid-paced, energetic discussion about the many similarities and differences between the two while the teacher lists them on the board.

71. The individual strategies the students will employ are:
    a. Collaborative learning and genre
    b. Brainstorming and a compare/contrast strategy
    c. Collaborative learning and brainstorming
    d. Analyzing and genre

72. The lesson is asking the students to consider two different:
    a. Learning styles
    b. Genres
    c. Writing styles
    d. Reading styles

73. The primary benefit of this exercise is that it promotes students':
    a. Vocabulary
    b. Comprehension
    c. Fluency
    d. Word identification

74. The students enjoyed the assignment so much that the teacher suggested they select one fairy tale and modernize it without changing the basic structure. Evil kings and queens could become corrupt politicians; pumpkins could turn into Hummers, and romantic princes might reveal themselves as rock stars. The teacher believes this assignment will most effectively demonstrate to the students:
    a. The importance of setting to meaning
    b. The importance of characters to meaning
    c. The importance of culture to meaning
    d. The importance of creativity to meaning

75. The first-grade teacher wants her class to understand that stories have a certain order. She reads them a story, then orally reviews with them how each event that happened in the story caused the next event to happen. To reinforce the lesson the teacher should:
   a. Give each child a piece of drawing paper that has been folded in half and then again, creating four boxes, along with a piece that has not been folded. The teacher should then ask the students to draw a cartoon about the story. Each of the first four boxes will show the events in order. The second page is to show how the story ends
   b. Give each child a piece of drawing paper and ask the students to draw the most important scene
   c. Give each child a piece of drawing paper and ask the students to draw the story's beginning on the front of the page and ending on the back
   d. Give each child a piece of drawing paper that has been folded in half and then again, creating four boxes, along with a piece that has not been folded. The teacher should then ask the students to draw a cartoon about anything they want. She reminds them to put their story cartoons in proper order

76. A ninth grade class is reading a 14-line poem in iambic pentameter. There are three stanzas of four lines each, and a two-line couplet at the end. Words at the end of each line rhyme with another word in the same stanza. The class is reading a:
   a. Sonnet
   b. Villanelle
   c. Sestina
   d. Limerick

77. A teacher is working with a group of English Language Learners. She asks them to take two pieces of paper. At the top of the first paper they are to write *SAME*, at the top of the other, *DIFFERENT*. Each child will consider what his native country and the United States have in common, and what distinct features each country possesses. The children are using which method in organizing their ideas?
   a. Hunt and peck
   b. Consider and persuade
   c. Evaluate and contrast
   d. Compare and contrast

78. Which student is most likely to need referral to a reading specialist for assessment, special instruction, or intervention?
   a. Annabel: a 2nd-grade student who tends to skip over words or phrases when she reads, affecting her comprehension of the text
   b. Cliff: a kindergarten student who is already reading simple chapter books with his parents at home or in class
   c. Noelle: a 1st-grader who avoids any activity in which she must read, both aloud and silently, preferring to ask an adult to read the text for her first
   d. Barrett: a 3rd-grader who often confuses the sounds of certain letters, such as /b/ and /d/ or /v/ and /u

79. Which assessment will determine a student's ability to identify initial, medial, blended, final, segmented, and manipulated 'units'?
    a. Phonological awareness assessment
    b. High-frequency word assessment
    c. Reading fluency assessment
    d. Comprehension quick-check

80. A third grader knows he needs to write from left to right and from top to bottom on the page. He knows what sounds are associated with specific letters. He can recognize individual letters and can hear word families. He correctly identifies prefixes, suffixes, and homonyms, and his reading comprehension is very good. However, when he is asked to write, he becomes very upset. He has trouble holding a pencil, his letters are very primitively executed, and his written work is not legible. He most likely has:
    a. Dysgraphia
    b. Dyslexia
    c. Dyspraxia
    d. Nonverbal learning disorder

81. The phrase "Pretty as a picture" is *best* described as a:
    a. Metaphor
    b. Cliché
    c. Simile
    d. Figure of speech

82. A fourth-grade teacher had her students write haiku in order to promote the students' _____.
    a. Reading comprehension
    b. Vocabulary
    c. Word identification skills
    d. Confidence

83. A second-grade teacher wants to help her students enrich their vocabulary. She's noticed that their writing journals are filled with serviceable but unexciting verbs such as "said" and "went," and general rather than specific nouns. The most effective lesson would involve:
    a. Suggesting students use a thesaurus to substitute more unusual words for common ones
    b. Suggesting students add an adjective to each noun
    c. Brainstorming a list of verbs that mean ways of talking or ways of going, then adding them to the word wall along with some nouns that specify common topics
    d. Suggesting students look up the meanings of boring words and consider another way to express them

84. Activating prior knowledge, shared reading, and using graphic organizers are all examples of what type of instructional concept?
    a. Modeling
    b. Scaffolding
    c. Assessing
    d. Inspiring

85. Examples of onomatopoeia are:
   a. Sink, drink, mink, link
   b. Their, there, they're
   c. Drip, chirp, splash, giggle
   d. *Think, in, thin, ink*

86. "Code knowledge" facilitates reading fluency because:
   a. It brings the entirety of the student's previous experience to bear on decoding a text
   b. It offers a framework for organizing new information by assigning code words to sets of ideas
   c. There is no such thing as "code knowledge." The correct term is "core knowledge"
   d. It offers a systematic approach to untangling the wide variety of vowel sounds when an unfamiliar word is encountered

87. The purpose of "targeted instruction" is to:
   a. Deliver instructions that are precise, clear, and direct so that students understand exactly what is expected
   b. Accurately rank a group of learners from low achievers to high achievers so that the teacher knows from the beginning of the school year which students have less ability and will therefore need support
   c. Teach students how to take information from a text and reorganize it into bulleted lists
   d. Assess and target areas needing improvement as well as areas of greatest strength for each student to ensure that all members of a class are receiving instruction tailored to their specific needs

88. Components of "explicit instruction" include:
   a. Clarifying the goal, modeling strategies, and offering explanations geared to a student's level of understanding
   b. Determining the goal, offering strategies, and asking questions designed to ascertain whether understanding has been reached
   c. Reassessing the goal, developing strategies, and determining whether further reassessing of the goal is required
   d. Objectifying the goal, assessing strategies, and offering explanations geared toward a student's level of understanding.

89. A teacher has challenged a student with a book about Antarctica that is just beyond the high end of the student's Instructional level. The teacher points out that the student already knows quite a bit about penguins because the class studied them earlier in the year. He reminds the student that she's recently seen a television show about the seals that also live in Antarctic waters. The teacher gives the student a list of words she's likely to find in the text, and they discuss what those words might mean. The student begins to read, but stops to ask the teacher what *circumpolar* means. The teacher is also unfamiliar with the word, but reminds her that *circum* is a prefix. The student recalls that it means "about or around" and deduces that circumpolar most likely refers to something found around or in a polar region. This instructional approach is called:
   a. Modular instruction
   b. Scaffolding
   c. Linking
   d. Transmutation

90. Which choice is <u>not</u> a cueing system used to understand unfamiliar words?
    a. Syntactic
    b. Semantic
    c. Graphophonic
    d. Auditory

91. An understanding of the meanings of prefixes and suffixes such as *dis, mis, un, re, able,* and *ment* are important for:
    a. Reading comprehension
    b. Word recognition
    c. Vocabulary building
    d. Reading fluency

92. VC, CVC, CCVC, CVCC, and CCVCC are among the types of:
    a. Homophones
    b. Closed syllables
    c. Monosyllabic words
    d. Polyglotal indicators

93. A student is taking a reading test. The teacher has blocked out a number of words. Each blank is assigned a set of three possible words. The student must select the correct word from each set so that the text makes sense. The student is taking:
    a. A cloze test
    b. A maze test
    c. A multiple-choice quiz
    d. A vocabulary test

94. When working with English Language Learners, the teacher should:
    a. Avoid idioms and slang, involve students in hands-on activities, reference students' prior knowledge, and speak slowly
    b. Speak slowly, use monosyllabic words whenever possible, repeat each sentence three times before moving to the next sentence, and employ idioms but not slang
    c. Use monosyllabic words whenever possible, repeat key instructions three times but not in a row, reference students' prior knowledge, and have students keep a journal of new vocabulary
    d. Have students keep a journal of new vocabulary, reference students' prior knowledge, speak slowly, and involve students in hands-on activities

95. Editing involves:
    a. Correcting surface features such as sentence fragments, spelling, and punctuation
    b. Fine-tuning the underlying structure of the piece to make the theme stand out
    c. Reconsidering ideas, adding or subtracting information, and changing the underlying structure
    d. Adding illustrations, charts, and other useful addenda

96. A seventh grader has never had much success with reading. Her ability to decode is rudimentary; she stops and starts when reading, frequently loses her place, or misreads an important word. She doesn't seem aware of where errors occur, or she does not attempt to correct them. When asked to tell about what she's read, her comprehension is minimal, to help her, instructional focus on which of the following would be most useful?
   a. Carefully organized lessons in decoding, sight words, vocabulary, and comprehension at least three to five times a week. These mini-lessons must be extremely clear, with the parts broken down to the lowest common denominator. The more tightly interwoven and systematized the instruction, the better chance this student will have
   b. A weekly lesson focusing on one aspect of reading. This student will be overwhelmed if too many strategies are offered at once. The instruction should focus first on recognizing sight words, then letter–sound association. Next, the girl needs an understanding of the rules of syntax.
   c. The student isn't trying. Her instruction should be aimed at helping her learn to be self-motivated and disciplined in her approach to learning
   d. Comprehension strategies will help her grasp the overall meaning of a text. From there she can begin to drill down until she's able to combine various approaches that, working together, will enable her to read

97. Silent reading fluency can best be assessed by:
   a. Having the student retell or summarize the material to determine how much was understood
   b. Giving a written test that covers plot, theme, character development, sequence of events, rising action, climax, falling action, and outcome. A student must test at a 95% accuracy rate to be considered fluent at silent reading
   c. Giving a three-minute Test of Silent Contextual Reading Fluency four times a year. The student is presented with text in which spaces between words and all punctuation have been removed. The student must divide one word from another with slash marks, as in the following example:
      The/little/sailboat/bobbed/so/far/in/the/distance/it/looked/like/a/toy. The more words a student accurately separates, the higher her silent reading fluency score
   d. Silent reading fluency cannot be assessed. It is a private act between the reader and the text and does not invite critique

98. A high school teacher has given her students an assignment to write a non-rhyming poem of three lines. The first and last lines each contain five syllables, and the middle line contains seven syllables. The students are writing a:
   a. Limerick
   b. Metaphor
   c. Villanelle
   d. Haiku

99. "Verbal dyspraxia" refers to:
   a. Trouble with the physical act of writing
   b. Confusing word or sentence order while speaking
   c. Misplacement of letters within words
   d. An inability to process verbal information

100. "Coarticulation" affects:
    a. Blending awareness
    b. Phonemic awareness
    c. Sequencing
    d. Aural awareness

Answers and Explanations

1. A: Homophones. Homophones are a type of homonym that sound alike, but are spelled differently and have different meanings. Other examples are *two, to,* and *too; their, they're,* and *there.*

2. C: Argumentative essay. The goal of a persuasive essay is to convince the reader that the author's position or opinion on a controversial topic is correct. That opinion or position is called the argument. A persuasive essay argues a series of points, supported by facts and evidence.

3. D: Rate, accuracy, and prosody. Fluent readers are able to read smoothly and comfortably at a steady pace (rate). The more quickly a child reads, the greater the chance of leaving out a word or substituting one word for another (for example, *sink* instead of *shrink*). Fluent readers are able to maintain accuracy without sacrificing rate. Fluent readers also stress important words in a text, group words into rhythmic phrases, and read with intonation (prosody).

4. B: The number of unrecognizable words an English Language Learner encounters when reading a passage or listening to a teacher. Language load is one of the barriers English Language Learners face. To lighten this load, a teacher can rephrase, eliminate unnecessary words, divide complex sentences into smaller units, and teach essential vocabulary before the student begins the lesson.

5. A: A vowel. A syllable is a minimal sound unit arranged around a vowel. For example, *academic* has four syllables: *a/ca/dem/ic.* It is possible for a syllable to be a single vowel, as in the above example. It is not possible for a syllable to be a single consonant.

6. C: Fail, producing students at a Frustration reading level. Those reading below grade level are likely to give up entirely. Those reading at grade level are likely to get frustrated and form habits that will actually slow down their development. Giving students texts that are too far beyond their reach produces frustrated readers. In an effort to succeed, frustrated writers are likely to apply strategies that have worked for them in the past but cannot work in this case because the text is simply beyond them. Looking for contextual clues to understand the meaning of unfamiliar words requires that most of the words in the passage are familiar. Breaking unfamiliar words into individual phonemes or syllables can be effective, but not if the number of such words is excessive. In this case, students below reading level and students at reading level will become frustrated when the skills that have worked for them in the past now fail.

7. C: Tier-two words. Tier-two words are words that are used with high frequency across a variety of disciplines or words with multiple meanings. They are characteristic of mature language users. Knowing these words is crucial to attaining an acceptable level of reading comprehension and communication skills.

8. C: Reading at her Independent reading level. When reading independently, students are at the correct level if they read with at least 97% accuracy.

9. B: To correct an error in reading a student has made, specifically clarifying where and how the error was made so that the student can avoid similar errors in the future. A reading teacher offers corrective feedback to a student in order to explain why a particular error in reading is, in fact, an error. Corrective feedback is specific; it locates where and how the student went astray so that similar errors can be avoided in future reading.

10. C: Content-specific words. Because these words are specific to paleontology, it's unlikely the students know their meanings. Without understanding what these words mean, the students would not be able to understand the content of the passage they were about to read.

11. B: Prior knowledge is knowledge the student brings from previous life or learning experiences to the act of reading. It is not possible for a student to fully comprehend new knowledge without first integrating it with prior knowledge. Prior knowledge, which rises from experience and previous learning, provides a framework by which new knowledge gained from the act of reading can be integrated. Every act of reading enriches a student's well of prior knowledge and increases that student's future ability to comprehend more fully any new knowledge acquired through reading.

12. B: Understanding of context and vocabulary. In a cloze test, a reader is given a text with certain words blocked out. The reader must be able to determine probable missing words based on contextual clues. In order to supply these words, the reader must already know them.

13. A: Common words with irregular spelling. Sight words occur in many types of writing; they are high-frequency words. Sight words are also words with irregular spelling. Some examples of sight words include *talk, some,* and *the.* Fluent readers need to recognize these words visually.

14. D: Consonant digraph. A consonant digraph is group of consonants in which all letters represent a single sound.

15. A: Phonological awareness. Phonemic awareness is the ability to recognize sounds within words. Segmenting words and blending sounds are components of phonemic awareness. Phonological awareness includes an understanding of multiple components of spoken language. Ability to hear individual words within a vocalized stream and ability to identify spoken syllables are types of phonological awareness.

16. A: Letter–sound correspondence. Letter–sound correspondence relies on the relationship between a spoken sound or group of sounds and the letters conventionally used in English to write them.

17. A: Strategy instruction. Strategic instruction involves teaching a methodic approach to solving a reading problem. It consists of strategies done in steps which aid the reader in eliminating incorrect responses.

18. D: Familiar, frequently used words that do not need to be taught beyond primary grades. Common or basic words are the first tier of three-tier words. These words are widely used across the spoken and written spectrum. Some examples are *walk, go, wish, the, look, happy,*

and *always.* This essential vocabulary is taught early in a reader's instruction, and beyond that it need not be taught.

19. B: The number of phonemes. A phoneme is the smallest measure of language sound. English language phonemes, about 40 in number, are composed of individual letters as well as letter combinations. A number of letters have more than one associated sound. For example, "c" can be pronounced as a hard "c" (cake) or a soft "c" (Cynthia). Vowels in particular have a number of possible pronunciations.

20. B: Consonant blend. Consonant blend refers to a group of consonants in which each letter represents a separate sound.

21. A: Fewer than 100 words in the time given. At the beginning of the school year, second-grade students should be able to read 50–80 words per minute. By the time they are well into the school year, second-grade-level reading is tracked at 85 words per minute.

22. D: None; sight words cannot be decoded. Readers must learn to recognize these words as wholes on sight. Sight words have irregular spelling. Segmenting them into syllables or using a phonemic approach are ineffective strategies to aid a reader in recognizing a sight word, because these approaches depend on rules a sight word doesn't follow. Word families group words that share common patterns of consonants and vowels. The spelling of those words is therefore regular, because they follow a predictable pattern. Sight words are irregular and do not follow a predictable pattern and must be instantaneously recognized for writing fluency. No decoding is useful.

23. D: It is impossible to include every text desired into the language curriculum—there are simply too many good books, stories, poems, speeches, and media available. Teachers must first think about what skills their students need to acquire, as well as what skills they have already mastered. In designing activities for class, a good teacher will start first with the purpose for instruction (or perceiving oral or visual text such as video or music). For example, purposes of reading can include: reading for information; reading for enjoyment; understanding a message; identifying main or supporting ideas; or developing an appreciation for artistic expression/perception. Once the purpose or intended learning outcome has been identified, the teacher will have a much better idea of which texts, strategies, and activities will support that purpose.

24. C: Alphabetic principle. The act of decoding involves first recognizing the sounds individual letters and letter groups make, and then blending the sounds to read the word. A child decoding the word *spin*, for example, would first pronounce *sp/i/n* as individual sound units. She then would repeat the sounds, smoothly blending them. Because decoding involves understanding letters and their sounds, it is sometimes known as the alphabetic principle.

25. C: Students can easily become bored or disinterested in reading if they are not exposed to a variety of reading texts. Also, reading can be overwhelming or frustrating for students who are still learning to read fluently or to comprehend what they read. By incorporating media, oral stories, and various types of print, students of all ability levels can build both fluency and comprehension skills. This approach also enables the teacher and students to discuss the relationship between all aspects of literacy, including speaking, listening, thinking, viewing, and reading.

26. A: Oral. Phonological awareness refers to an understanding of the sounds a word makes. While phonological awareness leads to fluent reading skills, activities designed to develop an awareness of word sounds are, by definition, oral.

27. B: Vocabulary. Strategizing in order to understand the meaning of a word, knowing multiple meanings of a single word, and applying background knowledge to glean a word's meaning are all ways in which an effective reader enhances vocabulary. Other skills include an awareness of word parts and word origins, the ability to apply word meanings in a variety of content areas, and a delight in learning the meanings of unfamiliar words.

28. C: She is reading at an Instructional level. In one minute, a student who misreads one or less than one word per twenty words, or with 95%–100% accuracy, is at an Independent reading level. A student who misreads one or less than one word per ten words, or with 90%–95% accuracy, is at an Instructional level. A student misreading more than one word out of ten, or with less than 90% accuracy, is at a Frustration level.

29. D: Decoding depends on an understanding of letter–sound relationships. As soon as a child understands enough letters and their correspondent sounds to read a few words, decoding should be introduced. The act of decoding involves first recognizing the sounds individual letters and letter groups in a word make and then blending the sounds to read the word. It's important to introduce the strategy as soon as a child knows enough letters and their corresponding sounds to read simple words.

30. C: Cause–effect words. Signal words give the reader hints about the purpose of a particular passage. Some signal words are concerned with comparing/contrasting, some with cause and effect, some with temporal sequencing, some with physical location, and some with a problem and its solution. The words *since, whether,* and *accordingly* are words used when describing an outcome. Outcomes have causes.

31. A: Outcome. Story action can be analyzed in terms of rising action, story climax, falling action, and resolution. Rising action consists of those events that occur before and lead up to the story's most dramatic moment, or climax. The climax occurs toward the end of the book, but rarely, if ever, right at the end. Following the climax, the consequences of that dramatic moment are termed falling action. The story reaches resolution with the outcome of the falling action.

32. C: Locate the vowels, then locate familiar word parts. Syllables are organized around vowels. In order to determine the syllables, this student should begin by locating the vowels. It's possible to have a syllable that is a single vowel (*a/gain*). It isn't possible to have a syllable that is a single consonant. Once the word has been broken into its component syllables the reader is able to study the syllables to find ones that are familiar and might give her a clue as to the word's meaning, such as certain prefixes or suffixes.

33. A: Nothing. These children are simply at an early stage in the reading/writing process. When emergent readers become aware of the connections between letters and sounds, and between reading and writing, they want to practice the skills they see proficient readers use. While a proficient writer knows that letters are grouped into words and that words are constructed into sentences that move from left to right and from the top of the page to the bottom, an emergent reader/writer knows only that letters magically contain sounds that other people can read. It is necessary for children to pass through early stages in which they

scribble-write and pretend they are scripting letters, which leads to a stage in which they actually do write the initial letter of a word all over the page. Next, the emergent reader/writer will write the initial letter of many of the words that belong in the sentence and will write them sequentially. KJM, for example, might mean *the cat chased a mouse.*

34. A: Scripting the end-sound to a word (KT=cat); leaving space between words; writing from the top left to the top right of the page, and from top to bottom. Each of these steps is progressively more abstract. Scripting the end-sound to a word helps a young writer recognize that words have beginnings and endings. This naturally leads to the willingness to separate words with white space so that they stand as individual entities. Once this step is reached, the child realizes that in English, writing progresses from left to right and from the top of the page to the bottom.

35. B: Ask the students to read their stories to her. Suggest they visit other children in the class and read to each of them. The teacher should encourage these students by "reading" what they have written, even if what she reads is incorrect. She might misread KJM as *Kathy jumped rope with Mandy.* Most children will not be upset by this, but will correct the teacher's misreading by reading what the letters really mean.

36. D: The teacher should encourage all students to "read" picture books from the first day of school. Talking about the pictures from page to page gives young readers the idea that books are arranged sequentially. Pictures also offer narrative coherence and contextual clues. Emergent readers who are encouraged to enjoy books will more readily embrace the act of reading. Holding a book and turning pages gives young readers a familiarity with them.

37. A: Most adults can understand the relationship between oral and written language: components of oral language have representational symbols that can be written and decoded. However, most normally-developing children acquire spoken language first and begin to develop reading and writing skills as they approach school-age. Many children are first exposed to the concept of written language when an adult introduces books or other written texts. However, a child's ability to read and write develops over time and is dependent on the development of physiological processes such as hearing, sight, and fine motor skills for writing. Written language development also typically requires direct instruction. Most children must be taught to read and write and rarely learn these skills simply by observing others.

38. C: Identify and use groups of letters that occur in a word family. Analogizing is based on recognizing the pattern of letters in words that share sound similarities. If the pattern is found at the end of a family of words, it is called a *rhyme*. Some examples of rhyme are *rent, sent, bent,* and *dent.* If the pattern is found at the beginning of the family of words, it is frequently a consonant *blend* such as *street, stripe,* or *strong,* in which all the letters are pronounced, or the pattern is a consonant digraph, in which the letters are taken together to represent a single sound such as in *phone, phonics,* or *phantom.*

39. A: Useful. The child will feel more confident because the story is already familiar. She will also feel that the lesson is a conversation of sorts, and that she is communicating successfully. She will be motivated to learn the English words because they are meaningful and highly charged. As a newly arrived immigrant, the child feels overwhelmed. Presenting her with a book of folk tales from her country tells her that she needn't lose her culture in

order to function in this one. It also comforts her by reminding her that her past and present are linked. Allowing her to speak in Korean helps her express herself without fear of judgment or failure. Presenting her with an English vocabulary that is meaningful ensures that she will eagerly embrace these words, her first words in her new language.

40. D: Cultural load. Cultural load is concerned with how the relationship between language and culture can help or hinder learning. By using the Korean folk tale, the teacher offered the child the opportunity to learn new words in a context that was culturally familiar. By demonstrating respect for her student's culture, she helped lighten the cultural load.

41. C: Right and left; left. Researchers have discovered through brain imaging that a dyslexic reader uses both sides of the brain. Non-dyslexic readers use only the left side.

42. B: Revising. Revision (literally, re+vision) is the act of "seeing again." When revising, writers examine what they have written in order to improve the meaning of the work. Fine-tuning word choices, moving information to another location, and adding or deleting words are all acts of revision.

43. D: Prefixes, appearing at the beginning of base words to change their meanings. Suffixes appear at the end of words. Prefixes are attached to the beginning of words to change their meanings. *Un+happy, bi+monthly,* and *re+examine* are prefixes that, by definition, change the meanings of the words to which they are attached.

44. D: Dog, sit, leg. CVC words are composed of a consonant, a vowel, and a consonant. To learn to read them, students must be familiar with the letters used and their sounds. A teacher can present a word like *sit* to students who also know the consonants *b/f/h/p* and ask them to create a word family of other CVC words. The students will be able to read *bit, fit, hit,* and *pit* because they are similar to the word *sit* they have just learned.

45. C: Context. By considering the other words in the story, the student can determine the missing words. The student is depending on the information supplied by the rest of the story. This information puts the story into context.

46. D: All of the above. Metacognition means a reader's awareness of her own reading processes as she improves reading comprehension. Other elements of metacognition include awareness of areas in the text where the reader fails to comprehend and an understanding of how the text is structured.

47. A: Cooperative learning and reading comprehension. Cooperative learning occurs when a group of students at various levels of reading ability have goals in common. Reading comprehension is achieved through reading both orally and silently, developing vocabulary, a reader's ability to predict what will occur in a piece of writing, a reader's ability to summarize the main points in a piece of writing, and a reader's ability to reflect on the text's meaning and connect that meaning to another text or personal experience.

48. B: Understanding the meaning of words that are not familiar. Context cues offer insight into the probable meaning of unfamiliar words.

49. C: Observe the child over the course of a week or two. Draw her into conversation and determine if her vocabulary is limited, if she displays emotional problems, or if her reticence could have another cause. Note how the child interacts with others in the class. Does she ever initiate conversation? If another child initiates, does she respond? Until the teacher monitors the child's verbal abilities and habits, she cannot determine if the lack of interaction suggests a learning disability, an emotional problem, or simply a shy personality. The teacher should informally observe the child over a period of time, noting if and when she initiates or responds to oral language, if she is reading with apparent comprehension, if her vocabulary is limited, and the degree to which the child is interested in understanding.

50. C: There are many genres from which students can choose to read. The most elemental distinction between genres consists of fiction and non-fiction, the latter referring to stories or texts that are true, or factual. Fictional texts can fall into a variety of categories. Realistic fiction seems as though it could be true. These stories involve realistic characters and settings with which readers can often identify. This type of fiction can treat different subjects, but it still must be relatable in nature.

51. C: Persuasive. The author is hoping to persuade or convince young readers to avoid sex by providing them with facts as well as by using rhetorical devices such as dispelling opposing arguments.

52. C: They meet to discuss areas the teacher is most concerned about and decide on the teacher's goals. In order to best achieve goals, those goals must be understood and established.

53. D: Being able to identify rhyme is an important element of phonological awareness. Young children use language in a solely oral way. Oral language is composed of separate sounds that are represented in written form by the alphabet. In order to read, a child must first have a sense of the sounds that are used in English (phonological awareness). By helping children hear the difference between rhyming and non-rhyming words, the teacher is preparing them to make the transition to sound–letter association and word families.

54. A: Closed, open, silent *e*, vowel team, vowel-*r*, and consonant-*le*. A closed syllable ends with a consonant, such as *cat*. Open syllables end with a vowel, such as *he*. Vowel team syllables contain two vowels working together, such as *main*. Vowel-*r* syllables such as *er* and *or* frequently occur as suffixes. Consonant-*le* syllables also typically occur as suffixes, such as *battle* or *terrible*.

55. A: Strategies to increase comprehension and to build vocabulary. The student should receive instruction focused on just those areas in which he is exhibiting difficulty. Improved vocabulary will give him greater skill at comprehending the meaning of a particular text. Strategies focused on enhancing comprehension together with a stronger vocabulary will provide the greatest help.

56. B: Through a combination of standardized testing, informal teacher observations, attention to grades, objective-linked assessments, and systematized charting of data over time. Reading comprehension and vocabulary cannot be sufficiently assessed with occasional, brief studies. Continuous observation, high-stakes and standardized testing, attention to grades, and closely tracking the outcomes of objective-linked assessments are

interrelated tools that, when systematically organized, offer a thorough understanding of students' strengths and weaknesses.

57. A: An Oral Reading Fluency assessment. ORF stands for oral reading fluency. This assessment measures the words correct per minute (WCPM) by subtracting the number of errors made from the total number of words orally read in a one- to two-minute period of time. It is used to find a student's Instructional reading level, to identify readers who are having difficulties, and to track developing fluency and word recognition over time.

58. D: Round-robin reading is a common practice in language arts classes and has been for many years. In this process, students take turns reading aloud for their peers. Other students are asked to follow along silently in their texts while a peer is reading. This strategy does provide a way for students to read texts in class and include as many students as possible, which is often the intended outcome. However, this process often creates a boring atmosphere, since only one student at a time is actively engaged. While that student is reading, other students may become distracted by their own thoughts, other school work, or off-task interaction with each another; all of these issues subvert the intended outcome of the process. There is rarely enough time for each student to practice reading aloud to build students' reading fluency or comprehension in significant ways.

59. D: Especially important to English Language Learners and students with reading disabilities. Word recognition is required for reading fluency and is important to all readers, but it is especially so to English Language Learners and students with reading disabilities. It can be effectively taught through precisely calibrated word study instruction designed to provide readers with reading and writing strategies for successful word analysis.

60. A: Proficiency with oral language enhances students' phonemic awareness and increases vocabulary. Understanding that words are scripted with specific letters representing specific sounds is essential to decoding a text. Students cannot effectively learn to read without the ability to decode. An enhanced vocabulary supports the act of reading; the larger an emergent reader's vocabulary, the more quickly he will learn to read. He will be able to decode more words, which he can organize into word families, which he can use to decode unfamiliar words.

61. C: Read the documents quickly, looking for key words in order to gather the basic premise of each. Skimming allows a reader to quickly gain a broad understanding of a piece of writing in order to determine if a more thorough reading is warranted. Skimming allows students who are researching a topic on the Internet or in print to consider a substantial body of information in order to select only that of particular relevance.

62. B: Expository. Expository essays clarify an idea, explain an event, or interpret facts. The position the author takes is often supported with statistics, quotations, or other evidence researched from a variety of sources.

63. B: Persuasive. A persuasive essay takes a strong position about a controversial topic and offers factual evidence to support this position. The goal of a persuasive paper is to convince the audience that the claim is true based on the evidence provided.

64. A: However, the myth of "safe cigarettes," questions about nicotine addiction, and denials about the dangers of secondhand smoke have proven to be propaganda and lies. A thesis statement offers a hypothesis or opinion that the remainder of the paper then sets out to prove. Oftentimes, the thesis statement also offers a clear road map of the paper, foreshadowing the focuses of the paragraphs that follow and the order in which they will appear.

65. D: The myth of "safe cigarettes," questions about nicotine addiction, and the dangers of secondhand smoke. These three foci are presented in the thesis statement in this order and will be fleshed out in the following three paragraphs as the body of the essay.

66. C: Example. Example essays, also called illustration essays, are simple, straightforward pieces that depend on clearly described examples to make their points. An example essay isn't trying to convince the reader (argumentative), compare similar or dissimilar things (compare/contrast), or point to relationships such as cause and effect. Often, example essays teach the reader how to accomplish something or about something.

67. C: Are homophones. Homophones are words that are pronounced the same, but differ in meaning. For example, a bride wears a 2 caret ring, but a horse eats a carrot.

68. A: Collaborative learning. A group of students working together on a project are applying numerous learning strategies at once. Collaborative learning is a hands-on approach that actively involves students in the learning process. Students involved in collaborative learning typically retain the lesson better.

69. C: Biography. A biography relates information about part of the life of an individual. An autobiography is a biography about the writer's own life. A memoir is also autobiographical, but focuses on a theme. Historical fiction uses a setting or event based in historical fact as the background for characters and/or action that is invented.

70. C: Students will do online research about the cultural, economic, or political events that were occurring during the specific time about which they've written. By researching the historic setting that cradled the events their interviewee discussed, students are simultaneously broadening their understanding of the context and working in a different content area.

71. B: Brainstorming and a compare/contrast strategy. Brainstorming is a prewriting activity in which an individual or group responds to a specific question by considering any and all responses that arise without editing, prioritizing, or selecting. Once the brainstorming session is complete, students look at the results and eliminate any responses that are not useful, then group and prioritize the remaining responses. In this example, the students are having a collaborative learning experience in that they are brainstorming together; however, collaborative learning is not a strategy per se, but is the outcome of a strategy. The students are also employing a compare/contrast strategy in that they are looking both at how the two writing styles share common elements and how they are distinct.

72. C: Writing styles. Both Anderson and the Grimms wrote in the same genre, that of fairy tales. Genre refers to types of writing. Mystery, romance, adventure, historical fiction, and fairy tales are some examples of genres. A genre can include many different authors and

writing styles. These students are being asked to compare two distinct writing styles within a single genre in order to locate similarities and differences.

73. B: Comprehension. This exercise requires students to examine the authors' use of setting, plot, pacing, word choice, syntactical structures, narration, mood, metaphors, point of view, voice, and character development to find ways in which they are similar as well as different. In so doing, the students are discovering that language shapes meaning in ways both subtle and profound.

74. C: The importance of culture to meaning. Authors make thousands of decisions in the act of writing. What point of view to take, how much weight to give an event, what to reveal about a character, and what words will most effectively express the writer's intention are but a few of these decisions. While many of these decisions are consciously artistic choices, many are unconscious and imbedded in the cultural expectations of time and place in which the author has lived. To understand a text to the fullest degree possible, it is necessary to read it with an eye to the cultural framework from whence it came.

75. A: Give each child a piece of drawing paper that has been folded in half and then again, creating four boxes, along with a piece that has not been folded. The teacher should then ask the students to draw a cartoon about the story. Each of the first four boxes will show the events in order. The second page is to show how the story ends. When a child is able to visually see the way a familiar story has unfolded, that child can find causal or thematic connections in the action that increases her comprehension of the story overall. Asking the class to draw a single picture or to draw the beginning and end doesn't sufficiently demonstrate the importance of order to meaning. While some first graders may be able to create their own cartoon stories that demonstrate a logical series of events, many first graders are not yet ready to organize thought into a linear progression.

76. A: Sonnet. There are three primary types of sonnets. The Shakespearean sonnet is specifically what these students are reading. A Spenserian sonnet is also composed of three four-line stanzas followed by a two-line couplet; however, the rhymes are not contained within each stanza but spill from one stanza to the next (*abab bcbc cdcd ee*). A Petrarchan sonnet divides into an eight-line stanza and a six-line stanza.

77. D: Compare and contrast. Asking children to write a list provides them with a visual model that is a side-by-side comparison of the two countries. In creating that visual model, each student first has to organize his or her thoughts mentally, deciding whether each particular item under consideration shares more or less in common with the other.

78. D: Teachers will observe a variety of developmental arcs when teaching reading, since all students learn differently. It is very important to understand which instances are normal in the course of learning and which signal a learning difficulty. Barrett is still exhibiting confusion over certain letter-sounds, typically when the letters look similar. At his age, this difficulty could suggest that Barrett has an issue with reading that could be addressed by a reading specialist. The other three choices describe normal behaviors that are commonly exhibited by children when they are learning to read. Choice C, Noelle, may describe an instance in which a student is having a learning problem. However, the teacher will need more information about Noelle's reading skills besides her reluctance to read before making a determination about how to proceed.

79. A: The words in this question prompt are most often used to refer to *sounds* made while reading. Initial/onset, medial, and final sounds are decoded in the beginning, middle, and end of words. When a teacher needs to assess an emergent or struggling reader's ability to differentiate between sounds in words, he or she may use a phonological awareness assessment. This tool will provide the teacher with information about the student's current ability to decode or encode words.

80. A: Dysgraphia. Dysgraphic individuals have difficulty with the physical act of writing. They find holding and manipulating a pencil problematic. Their letters are primitively formed, and their handwriting is illegible.

81. B: Cliché. While "Pretty as a picture" is a simile (comparison of two unlike things using *like* or *as*), its overuse has turned it into a cliché. A cliché is a trite platitude.

82. B: Vocabulary. The tightly controlled syllabic requirements will cause students to search for words outside their normal vocabularies that will fit the rigid framework and still express the writer's intended meanings. Often, students will rediscover a word whose meaning they know, but they don't often use.

83. C: Brainstorming a list of verbs that mean ways of talking or ways of going, then adding them to the word wall along with some nouns that specify common topics. Second graders aren't developmentally ready for a thesaurus; most will believe that any words in a particular list are interchangeable. For example, a student who wrote *my little sister walks like a baby* might find the verbs *strut, sidle,* and *amble* in the thesaurus. None of these verbs would be an appropriate substitution. Supplementing a noun with an adjective often results in flat writing: *There's a tree in my yard* might become *There's a nice tree in my big yard.* Adjectives such as *pretty, fun, cute, funny,* and so forth don't add much in terms of meaning, but they are the adjectives younger writers reach for first. A more specific noun is both more meaningful and more interesting. *There's a weeping willow in my yard* is evocative.

84. B: Scaffolding refers to any kind of special instruction designed to help students learn a new or challenging concept. There are countless forms of scaffolding techniques. The three techniques mentioned in the question prompt are all used to facilitate student understanding of a given text or a concept taught within the text. Scaffolding should not be confused with modeling strategies, which refer to the process of demonstrating how something should be done before a student tries it on his or her own.

85. C: *Drip, chirp, splash, giggle*. Onomatopoeia refers to words that sound like what they represent.

86. D: It offers a systematic approach to untangling the wide variety of vowel sounds when an unfamiliar word is encountered. Code knowledge, also called orthographic tendencies, is a helpful approach to decoding a word when multiple pronunciation possibilities exist. Example in the words *toe, go, though,* and *low*, the long O sound is written in a variety of ways. A code knowledge approach teaches a reader to first try a short vowel sound. If that doesn't help, the reader should consider the different ways the vowel or vowel groups can be pronounced, based on what he knows about other words.

87. D: Assess and target areas needing improvement as well as areas of greatest strength for each student to ensure that all members of a class are receiving instruction tailored to their specific needs.

88. A: Clarifying the goal, modeling strategies, and offering explanations geared to a student's level of understanding. Explicit instruction is well organized and structured, and it offers easily understood steps and depends in part on frequent reference to previously learned materials.

89. B: Scaffolding. Using this strategic approach, a teacher assigns a task that is just beyond the student's current level. The teacher encourages the student's attempts at comprehension by offering various supports that largely depend on prior knowledge, in order to develop the student's willingness to move forward into uncharted territory as a confident independent learner.

90. D: There are various cueing systems that readers can use to help them understand how to read or comprehend unfamiliar words. Semantic cueing helps with understanding word meaning; the reader uses the meaning of the words around an unfamiliar word to understand what that word means. Syntactical cueing can also be called "grammatical cueing," in which a reader uses the syntax of a sentence to understand more about an unfamiliar word. Graphophonic cueing is most useful in decoding, or breaking words down into smaller components new words.

91. A: Reading comprehension. Prefixes and suffixes change the meanings of the root word to which they are attached. A student who understands that *un* means "not" will be able to decipher the meanings of words such as *unwanted, unhappy,* or *unreasonable.*

92. B: Closed syllables. Closed syllables are those that end with a consonant. *At, dog, spit, duck,* and *pluck* are all examples of closed syllables.

93. B: A maze test. A maze test is a specific type of cloze test. In a cloze test, words are deleted and the reader must supply the missing words using contextual clues and vocabulary that is familiar. A maze test is a multiple-choice application of a cloze test.

94. A: Avoid idioms and slang, involve students in hands-on activities, reference students' prior knowledge, and speak slowly. Teachers of English Language Learners should not employ idioms and slang in their instruction because these informal uses of speech are likely to confuse the students. Involving students in hands-on activities such as group reading and language play makes the experience both more meaningful and more immediate. New knowledge can only be absorbed by attaching it to prior knowledge, referencing what students already know is essential. Speaking slowly to English Language Learners is important, because they are processing what is being said at a slower rate than a native speaker.

95. A: Correcting surface features such as sentence fragments, spelling, and punctuation. Editing is the final step in the writing process. The writer has already decided the ideas or events are in proper order, have been sufficiently described, and are clear. Now the writer turns her attention to surface features, "scrubbing" errors in spelling, punctuation, and syntax from the writing.

96. A: Carefully organized lessons in decoding, sight words, vocabulary, and comprehension at least three to five times a week. These mini-lessons must be extremely clear, with the parts broken down to the lowest common denominator. The more tightly interwoven and systematized the instruction, the better chance this student will have. This type of learner needs, first and foremost, instruction that has been highly organized into a system that will make sense to her. If possible, she should receive private instruction on a daily basis. The instruction needs to focus on decoding, recognizing words, reading with increasing fluency, enhancing vocabulary, and comprehension. She should be working at the Instructional level, or with texts she can read with at least 90% accuracy.

97. C: Giving a three-minute Test of Silent Contextual Reading Fluency four times a year. The student is presented with text in which spaces between words and all punctuation have been removed. The student must divide one word from another with slash marks, as in the following example: *The/little/sailboat/bobbed/so/far/in/the/distance/it/looked/like/a/toy*. The more words a student accurately separates, then the higher her silent reading fluency score. Silent reading fluency can be monitored over time by giving the Test of Silent Contextual Reading Fluency (TSCRF) four times a year. A similar assessment tool is the Test of Silent Word Reading Fluency (TOSWRF), in which words of increasing complexity are given as a single, undifferentiated, and unpunctuated strand. As with the TSCRF, three minutes are given for the student to separate each word from the next. *Itwillcannotschoolbecomeagendaconsistentphilosophysuperfluous* is an example of such a strand.

98. D: Haiku. Based on a Japanese form of poetry, haiku have become popular with students and teachers alike. Reading and writing haiku helps younger students become aware of syllables and helps older students learn about subtleties of vocabulary.

99. B: Confusing word or sentence order while speaking. Dyspraxic individuals do not process spoken language sequentially due to a neurological distortion. The dislocation of sounds within a word, such as vocalizing *lamp* instead of *palm*, is one indication of verbal dyspraxia.

100. B: Phonemic awareness. Vocalizing words involves arranging a series of continuous, voice, unvoiced, and stop sounds. As one sound is being uttered, the tongue and lips are already assuming the shape required by the next sound in the word. This process, which is not conscious, can distort individual sounds. One sound can slur into another, clip the end of the previous sound, or flatten or heighten a sound. For children who have difficulty hearing distinct phonemic sounds, individual instruction may be required.

Secret Key #1 - Time is Your Greatest Enemy

Pace Yourself

Wear a watch. At the beginning of the test, check the time (or start a chronometer on your watch to count the minutes), and check the time after every few questions to make sure you are "on schedule."

If you are forced to speed up, do it efficiently. Usually one or more answer choices can be eliminated without too much difficulty. Above all, don't panic. Don't speed up and just begin guessing at random choices. By pacing yourself, and continually monitoring your progress against your watch, you will always know exactly how far ahead or behind you are with your available time. If you find that you are one minute behind on the test, don't skip one question without spending any time on it, just to catch back up. Take 15 fewer seconds on the next four questions, and after four questions you'll have caught back up. Once you catch back up, you can continue working each problem at your normal pace.

Furthermore, don't dwell on the problems that you were rushed on. If a problem was taking up too much time and you made a hurried guess, it must be difficult. The difficult questions are the ones you are most likely to miss anyway, so it isn't a big loss. It is better to end with more time than you need than to run out of time.

Lastly, sometimes it is beneficial to slow down if you are constantly getting ahead of time. You are always more likely to catch a careless mistake by working more slowly than quickly, and among very high-scoring test takers (those who are likely to have lots of time left over), careless errors affect the score more than mastery of material.

Secret Key #2 - Guessing is not Guesswork

You probably know that guessing is a good idea. Unlike other standardized tests, there is no penalty for getting a wrong answer. Even if you have no idea about a question, you still have a 20-25% chance of getting it right.

Most test takers do not understand the impact that proper guessing can have on their score. Unless you score extremely high, guessing will significantly contribute to your final score.

Monkeys Take the Test

What most test takers don't realize is that to insure that 20-25% chance, you have to guess randomly. If you put 20 monkeys in a room to take this test, assuming they answered once per question and behaved themselves, on average they would get 20-25% of the questions correct. Put 20 test takers in the room, and the average will be much lower among guessed questions. Why?

1. The test writers intentionally write deceptive answer choices that "look" right. A test taker has no idea about a question, so he picks the "best looking" answer, which is often wrong. The monkey has no idea what looks good and what doesn't, so it will consistently be right about 20-25% of the time.
2. Test takers will eliminate answer choices from the guessing pool based on a hunch or intuition. Simple but correct answers often get excluded, leaving a 0% chance of being correct. The monkey has no clue, and often gets lucky with the best choice.

This is why the process of elimination endorsed by most test courses is flawed and detrimental to your performance. Test takers don't guess; they make an ignorant stab in the dark that is usually worse than random.

$5 Challenge

Let me introduce one of the most valuable ideas of this course—the $5 challenge:

You only mark your "best guess" if you are willing to bet $5 on it.
You only eliminate choices from guessing if you are willing to bet $5 on it.

Why $5? Five dollars is an amount of money that is small yet not insignificant, and can really add up fast (20 questions could cost you $100). Likewise, each answer choice on one question of the test will have a small impact on your overall score, but it can really add up to a lot of points in the end.

The process of elimination IS valuable. The following shows your chance of guessing it right:

If you eliminate wrong answer choices until only this many remain:	Chance of getting it correct:
1	100%
2	50%
3	33%

However, if you accidentally eliminate the right answer or go on a hunch for an incorrect answer, your chances drop dramatically—to 0%. By guessing among all the answer choices, you are GUARANTEED to have a shot at the right answer.

That's why the $5 test is so valuable. If you give up the advantage and safety of a pure guess, it had better be worth the risk.

What we still haven't covered is how to be sure that whatever guess you make is truly random. Here's the easiest way:

Always pick the first answer choice among those remaining.

Such a technique means that you have decided, **before you see a single test question**, exactly how you are going to guess, and since the order of choices tells you nothing about which one is correct, this guessing technique is perfectly random.

This section is not meant to scare you away from making educated guesses or eliminating choices; you just need to define when a choice is worth eliminating. The $5 test, along with a pre-defined random guessing strategy, is the best way to make sure you reap all of the benefits of guessing.

Secret Key #3 - Practice Smarter, Not Harder

Many test takers delay the test preparation process because they dread the awful amounts of practice time they think necessary to succeed on the test. We have refined an effective method that will take you only a fraction of the time.

There are a number of "obstacles" in the path to success. Among these are answering questions, finishing in time, and mastering test-taking strategies. All must be executed on the day of the test at peak performance, or your score will suffer. The test is a mental marathon that has a large impact on your future.

Just like a marathon runner, it is important to work your way up to the full challenge. So first you just worry about questions, and then time, and finally strategy:

Success Strategy

1. Find a good source for practice tests.
2. If you are willing to make a larger time investment, consider using more than one study guide. Often the different approaches of multiple authors will help you "get" difficult concepts.
3. Take a practice test with no time constraints, with all study helps, "open book." Take your time with questions and focus on applying strategies.
4. Take a practice test with time constraints, with all guides, "open book."
5. Take a final practice test without open material and with time limits.

If you have time to take more practice tests, just repeat step 5. By gradually exposing yourself to the full rigors of the test environment, you will condition your mind to the stress of test day and maximize your success.

Secret Key #4 - Prepare, Don't Procrastinate

Let me state an obvious fact: if you take the test three times, you will probably get three different scores. This is due to the way you feel on test day, the level of preparedness you have, and the version of the test you see. Despite the test writers' claims to the contrary, some versions of the test WILL be easier for you than others.

Since your future depends so much on your score, you should maximize your chances of success. In order to maximize the likelihood of success, you've got to prepare in advance. This means taking practice tests and spending time learning the information and test taking strategies you will need to succeed.

Never go take the actual test as a "practice" test, expecting that you can just take it again if you need to. Take all the practice tests you can on your own, but when you go to take the official test, be prepared, be focused, and do your best the first time!

Secret Key #5 - Test Yourself

Everyone knows that time is money. There is no need to spend too much of your time or too little of your time preparing for the test. You should only spend as much of your precious time preparing as is necessary for you to get the score you need.

Once you have taken a practice test under real conditions of time constraints, then you will know if you are ready for the test or not.

If you have scored extremely high the first time that you take the practice test, then there is not much point in spending countless hours studying. You are already there.

Benchmark your abilities by retaking practice tests and seeing how much you have improved. Once you consistently score high enough to guarantee success, then you are ready.

If you have scored well below where you need, then knuckle down and begin studying in earnest. Check your improvement regularly through the use of practice tests under real conditions. Above all, don't worry, panic, or give up. The key is perseverance!

Then, when you go to take the test, remain confident and remember how well you did on the practice tests. If you can score high enough on a practice test, then you can do the same on the real thing.

General Strategies

The most important thing you can do is to ignore your fears and jump into the test immediately. Do not be overwhelmed by any strange-sounding terms. You have to jump into the test like jumping into a pool—all at once is the easiest way.

Make Predictions

As you read and understand the question, try to guess what the answer will be. Remember that several of the answer choices are wrong, and once you begin reading them, your mind will immediately become cluttered with answer choices designed to throw you off. Your mind is typically the most focused immediately after you have read the question and digested its contents. If you can, try to predict what the correct answer will be. You may be surprised at what you can predict.

Quickly scan the choices and see if your prediction is in the listed answer choices. If it is, then you can be quite confident that you have the right answer. It still won't hurt to check the other answer choices, but most of the time, you've got it!

Answer the Question

It may seem obvious to only pick answer choices that answer the question, but the test writers can create some excellent answer choices that are wrong. Don't pick an answer just because it sounds right, or you believe it to be true. It MUST answer the question. Once you've made your selection, always go back and check it against the question and make sure that you didn't misread the question and that the answer choice does answer the question posed.

Benchmark

After you read the first answer choice, decide if you think it sounds correct or not. If it doesn't, move on to the next answer choice. If it does, mentally mark that answer choice. This doesn't mean that you've definitely selected it as your answer choice, it just means that it's the best you've seen thus far. Go ahead and read the next choice. If the next choice is worse than the one you've already selected, keep going to the next answer choice. If the next choice is better than the choice you've already selected, mentally mark the new answer choice as your best guess.

The first answer choice that you select becomes your standard. Every other answer choice must be benchmarked against that standard. That choice is correct until proven otherwise by another answer choice beating it out. Once you've decided that no other answer choice seems as good, do one final check to ensure that your answer choice answers the question posed.

Valid Information

Don't discount any of the information provided in the question. Every piece of information may be necessary to determine the correct answer. None of the information in the question is there to throw you off (while the answer choices will certainly have information to throw you off). If two seemingly unrelated topics are discussed, don't ignore either. You can be confident there is a relationship, or it wouldn't be included in the question, and you are probably going to have to determine what is that relationship to find the answer.

Avoid "Fact Traps"

Don't get distracted by a choice that is factually true. Your search is for the answer that answers the question. Stay focused and don't fall for an answer that is true but irrelevant. Always go back to the question and make sure you're choosing an answer that actually answers the question and is not just a true statement. An answer can be factually correct, but it MUST answer the question asked. Additionally, two answers can both be seemingly correct, so be sure to read all of the answer choices, and make sure that you get the one that BEST answers the question.

Milk the Question

Some of the questions may throw you completely off. They might deal with a subject you have not been exposed to, or one that you haven't reviewed in years. While your lack of knowledge about the subject will be a hindrance, the question itself can give you many clues that will help you find the correct answer. Read the question carefully and look for clues.

Watch particularly for adjectives and nouns describing difficult terms or words that you don't recognize. Regardless of whether you completely understand a word or not, replacing it with a synonym, either provided or one you more familiar with, may help you to understand what the questions are asking. Rather than wracking your mind about specific detailed information concerning a difficult term or word, try to use mental substitutes that are easier to understand.

The Trap of Familiarity

Don't just choose a word because you recognize it. On difficult questions, you may not recognize a number of words in the answer choices. The test writers don't put "make-believe" words on the test, so don't think that just because you only recognize all the words in one answer choice that that answer choice must be correct. If you only recognize words in one answer choice, then focus on that one. Is it correct? Try your best to determine if it is correct. If it is, that's great. If not, eliminate it. Each word and answer choice you eliminate increases your chances of getting the question correct, even if you then have to guess among the unfamiliar choices.

Eliminate Answers

Eliminate choices as soon as you realize they are wrong. But be careful! Make sure you consider all of the possible answer choices. Just because one appears right, doesn't mean that the next one won't be even better! The test writers will usually put more than one good answer choice for every question, so read all of them. Don't worry if you are stuck between two that seem right. By getting down to just two remaining possible choices, your odds are now 50/50. Rather than wasting too much time, play the odds. You are guessing, but guessing wisely because you've been able to knock out some of the answer choices that you know are wrong. If you are eliminating choices and realize that the last answer choice you are left with is also obviously wrong, don't panic. Start over and consider each choice again. There may easily be something that you missed the first time and will realize on the second pass.

Tough Questions

If you are stumped on a problem or it appears too hard or too difficult, don't waste time. Move on! Remember though, if you can quickly check for obviously incorrect answer choices, your chances of guessing correctly are greatly improved. Before you completely give up, at least try to knock out a couple of possible answers. Eliminate what you can and then guess at the remaining answer choices before moving on.

Brainstorm

If you get stuck on a difficult question, spend a few seconds quickly brainstorming. Run through the complete list of possible answer choices. Look at each choice and ask yourself, "Could this answer the question satisfactorily?" Go through each answer choice and consider it independently of the others. By systematically going through all possibilities, you may find something that you would otherwise overlook. Remember though that when you get stuck, it's important to try to keep moving.

Read Carefully

Understand the problem. Read the question and answer choices carefully. Don't miss the question because you misread the terms. You have plenty of time to read each question thoroughly and make sure you understand what is being asked. Yet a happy medium must be attained, so don't waste too much time. You must read carefully, but efficiently.

Face Value

When in doubt, use common sense. Always accept the situation in the problem at face value. Don't read too much into it. These problems will not require you to make huge leaps of logic. The test writers aren't trying to throw you off with a cheap trick. If you have to go beyond creativity and make a leap of logic in order to have an answer choice answer the question, then you should look at the other answer choices. Don't overcomplicate the problem by creating theoretical relationships or explanations that will warp time or space. These are normal problems rooted in reality. It's just that the applicable relationship or explanation may not be readily apparent and you have to figure things out. Use your common sense to interpret anything that isn't clear.

Prefixes

If you're having trouble with a word in the question or answer choices, try dissecting it. Take advantage of every clue that the word might include. Prefixes and suffixes can be a huge help. Usually they allow you to determine a basic meaning. Pre- means before, post- means after, pro - is positive, de- is negative. From these prefixes and suffixes, you can get an idea of the general meaning of the word and try to put it into context. Beware though of any traps. Just because con- is the opposite of pro-, doesn't necessarily mean congress is the opposite of progress!

Hedge Phrases

Watch out for critical hedge phrases, led off with words such as "likely," "may," "can," "sometimes," "often," "almost," "mostly," "usually," "generally," "rarely," and "sometimes." Question writers insert these hedge phrases to cover every possibility. Often an answer choice will be wrong simply because it leaves no room for exception. Unless the situation calls for them, avoid answer choices that have definitive words like "exactly," and "always."

Switchback Words

Stay alert for "switchbacks." These are the words and phrases frequently used to alert you to shifts in thought. The most common switchback word is "but." Others include "although," "however," "nevertheless," "on the other hand," "even though," "while," "in spite of," "despite," and "regardless of."

New Information

Correct answer choices will rarely have completely new information included. Answer choices typically are straightforward reflections of the material asked about and will directly relate to the question. If a new piece of information is included in an answer choice that doesn't even seem to relate to the topic being asked about, then that answer choice is likely incorrect. All of the information needed to answer the question is usually provided for you in the question. You should not have to make guesses that are unsupported or choose answer choices that require unknown information that cannot be reasoned from what is given.

Time Management

On technical questions, don't get lost on the technical terms. Don't spend too much time on any one question. If you don't know what a term means, then odds are you aren't going to get much further since you don't have a dictionary. You should be able to immediately recognize whether or not you know a term.

If you don't, work with the other clues that you have—the other answer choices and terms provided—but don't waste too much time trying to figure out a difficult term that you don't know.

Contextual Clues

Look for contextual clues. An answer can be right but not the correct answer. The contextual clues will help you find the answer that is most right and is correct. Understand the context in which a phrase or statement is made. This will help you make important distinctions.

Don't Panic

Panicking will not answer any questions for you; therefore, it isn't helpful. When you first see the question, if your mind goes blank, take a deep breath. Force yourself to mechanically go through the steps of solving the problem using the strategies you've learned.

Pace Yourself

Don't get clock fever. It's easy to be overwhelmed when you're looking at a page full of questions, your mind is full of random thoughts and feeling confused, and the clock is ticking down faster than you would like. Calm down and maintain the pace that you have set for yourself. As long as you are on track by monitoring your pace, you are guaranteed to have enough time for yourself. When you get to the last few minutes of the test, it may seem like you won't have enough time left, but if you only have as many questions as you should have left at that point, then you're right on track!

Answer Selection

The best way to pick an answer choice is to eliminate all of those that are wrong, until only one is left and confirm that is the correct answer. Sometimes though, an answer choice may immediately look right. Be careful! Take a second to make sure that the other choices are not equally obvious. Don't make a hasty mistake. There are only two times that you should stop before checking other answers. First is when you are positive that the answer choice you have selected is correct. Second is when time is almost out and you have to make a quick guess!

Check Your Work

Since you will probably not know every term listed and the answer to every question, it is important that you get credit for the ones that you do know. Don't miss any questions through careless mistakes. If at all possible, try to take a second to look back over your answer selection and make sure you've selected the correct answer choice and haven't made a costly careless mistake (such as marking an answer choice that you didn't mean to mark). The time it takes for this quick double check should more than pay for itself in caught mistakes.

Beware of Directly Quoted Answers

Sometimes an answer choice will repeat word for word a portion of the question or reference section. However, beware of such exact duplication. It may be a trap! More than likely, the correct choice will paraphrase or summarize a point, rather than being exactly the same wording.

Slang

Scientific sounding answers are better than slang ones. An answer choice that begins "To compare the outcomes..." is much more likely to be correct than one that begins "Because some people insisted..."

Extreme Statements

Avoid wild answers that throw out highly controversial ideas that are proclaimed as established fact. An answer choice that states the "process should used in certain situations, if..." is much more likely to be correct than one that states the "process should be discontinued completely." The first is a calm rational statement and doesn't even make a definitive, uncompromising stance, using a hedge word "if" to provide wiggle room, whereas the second choice is a radical idea and far more extreme.

Answer Choice Families

When you have two or more answer choices that are direct opposites or parallels, one of them is usually the correct answer. For instance, if one answer choice states "x increases" and another answer choice states "x decreases" or "y increases," then those two or three answer choices are very similar in construction and fall into the same family of answer choices. A family of answer choices consists of two or three answer choices, very similar in construction, but often with directly opposite meanings. Usually the correct answer choice will be in that family of answer choices. The "odd man out" or answer choice that doesn't seem to fit the parallel construction of the other answer choices is more likely to be incorrect.

Special Report: How to Overcome Test Anxiety

The very nature of tests caters to some level of anxiety, nervousness, or tension, just as we feel for any important event that occurs in our lives. A little bit of anxiety or nervousness can be a good thing. It helps us with motivation, and makes achievement just that much sweeter. However, too much anxiety can be a problem, especially if it hinders our ability to function and perform.

"Test anxiety," is the term that refers to the emotional reactions that some test-takers experience when faced with a test or exam. Having a fear of testing and exams is based upon a rational fear, since the test-taker's performance can shape the course of an academic career. Nevertheless, experiencing excessive fear of examinations will only interfere with the test-taker's ability to perform and chance to be successful.

There are a large variety of causes that can contribute to the development and sensation of test anxiety. These include, but are not limited to, lack of preparation and worrying about issues surrounding the test.

Lack of Preparation

Lack of preparation can be identified by the following behaviors or situations:

Not scheduling enough time to study, and therefore cramming the night before the test or exam
Managing time poorly, to create the sensation that there is not enough time to do everything
Failing to organize the text information in advance, so that the study material consists of the entire text and not simply the pertinent information
Poor overall studying habits

Worrying, on the other hand, can be related to both the test taker, or many other factors around him/her that will be affected by the results of the test. These include worrying about:

Previous performances on similar exams, or exams in general
How friends and other students are achieving
The negative consequences that will result from a poor grade or failure

There are three primary elements to test anxiety. Physical components, which involve the same typical bodily reactions as those to acute anxiety (to be discussed below). Emotional factors have to do with fear or panic. Mental or cognitive issues concerning attention spans and memory abilities.

Physical Signals

There are many different symptoms of test anxiety, and these are not limited to mental and emotional strain. Frequently there are a range of physical signals that will let a test taker know that he/she is suffering from test anxiety. These bodily changes can include the following:

Perspiring
Sweaty palms
Wet, trembling hands
Nausea
Dry mouth
A knot in the stomach
Headache
Faintness
Muscle tension
Aching shoulders, back and neck
Rapid heart beat
Feeling too hot/cold

To recognize the sensation of test anxiety, a test-taker should monitor him/herself for the following sensations:

The physical distress symptoms as listed above
Emotional sensitivity, expressing emotional feelings such as the need to cry or laugh too much, or a sensation of anger or helplessness
A decreased ability to think, causing the test-taker to blank out or have racing thoughts that are hard to organize or control.

Though most students will feel some level of anxiety when faced with a test or exam, the majority can cope with that anxiety and maintain it at a manageable level. However, those who cannot are faced with a very real and very serious condition, which can and should be controlled for the immeasurable benefit of this sufferer.

Naturally, these sensations lead to negative results for the testing experience. The most common effects of test anxiety have to do with nervousness and mental blocking.

Nervousness

Nervousness can appear in several different levels:

The test-taker's difficulty, or even inability to read and understand the questions on the test
The difficulty or inability to organize thoughts to a coherent form
The difficulty or inability to recall key words and concepts relating to the testing questions (especially essays)
The receipt of poor grades on a test, though the test material was well known by the test taker

Conversely, a person may also experience mental blocking, which involves:

Blanking out on test questions
Only remembering the correct answers to the questions when the test has already finished.

Fortunately for test anxiety sufferers, beating these feelings, to a large degree, has to do with proper preparation. When a test taker has a feeling of preparedness, then anxiety will be dramatically lessened.

The first step to resolving anxiety issues is to distinguish which of the two types of anxiety are being suffered. If the anxiety is a direct result of a lack of preparation, this should be considered a normal reaction, and the anxiety level (as opposed to the test results) shouldn't be anything to worry about. However, if, when adequately prepared, the test-taker still panics, blanks out, or seems to overreact, this is not a fully rational reaction. While this can be considered normal too, there are many ways to combat and overcome these effects.

Remember that anxiety cannot be entirely eliminated, however, there are ways to minimize it, to make the anxiety easier to manage. Preparation is one of the best ways to minimize test anxiety. Therefore the following techniques are wise in order to best fight off any anxiety that may want to build.

To begin with, try to avoid cramming before a test, whenever it is possible. By trying to memorize an entire term's worth of information in one day, you'll be shocking your system, and not giving yourself a very good chance to absorb the information. This is an easy path to anxiety, so for those who suffer from test anxiety, cramming should not even be considered an option.

Instead of cramming, work throughout the semester to combine all of the material which is presented throughout the semester, and work on it gradually as the course goes by, making sure to master the main concepts first, leaving minor details for a week or so before the test.

To study for the upcoming exam, be sure to pose questions that may be on the examination, to gauge the ability to answer them by integrating the ideas from your texts, notes and lectures, as well as any supplementary readings.

If it is truly impossible to cover all of the information that was covered in that particular term, concentrate on the most important portions, that can be covered very well. Learn these concepts as best as possible, so that when the test comes, a goal can be made to use these concepts as presentations of your knowledge.

In addition to study habits, changes in attitude are critical to beating a struggle with test anxiety. In fact, an improvement of the perspective over the entire test-taking experience can actually help a test taker to enjoy studying and therefore improve the overall experience. Be certain not to overemphasize the significance of the grade - know that the result of the test is neither a reflection of self worth, nor is it a measure of intelligence; one grade will not predict a person's future success.

To improve an overall testing outlook, the following steps should be tried:

Keeping in mind that the most reasonable expectation for taking a test is to expect to try to demonstrate as much of what you know as you possibly can.
Reminding ourselves that a test is only one test; this is not the only one, and there will be others.
The thought of thinking of oneself in an irrational, all-or-nothing term should be avoided at all costs.
A reward should be designated for after the test, so there's something to look forward to. Whether it be going to a movie, going out to eat, or simply visiting friends, schedule it in advance, and do it no matter what result is expected on the exam.

Test-takers should also keep in mind that the basics are some of the most important things, even beyond anti-anxiety techniques and studying. Never neglect the basic social, emotional and biological needs, in order to try to absorb information. In order to best achieve, these three factors must be held as just as important as the studying itself.

Study Steps

Remember the following important steps for studying:

Maintain healthy nutrition and exercise habits. Continue both your recreational activities and social pass times. These both contribute to your physical and emotional well being.
Be certain to get a good amount of sleep, especially the night before the test, because when you're overtired you are not able to perform to the best of your best ability.
Keep the studying pace to a moderate level by taking breaks when they are needed, and varying the work whenever possible, to keep the mind fresh instead of getting bored. When enough studying has been done that all the material that can be learned has been learned, and the test taker is prepared for the test, stop studying and do something relaxing such as listening to music, watching a movie, or taking a warm bubble bath.

There are also many other techniques to minimize the uneasiness or apprehension that is experienced along with test anxiety before, during, or even after the examination. In fact, there are a great deal of things that can be done to stop anxiety from interfering with lifestyle and performance. Again, remember that anxiety will not be eliminated entirely, and it shouldn't be. Otherwise that "up" feeling for exams would not exist, and most of us depend on that sensation to perform better than usual. However, this anxiety has to be at a level that is manageable.

Of course, as we have just discussed, being prepared for the exam is half the battle right away. Attending all classes, finding out what knowledge will be expected on the exam, and knowing the exam schedules are easy steps to lowering anxiety. Keeping up with work will remove the need to cram, and efficient study habits will eliminate wasted time. Studying should be done in an ideal location for concentration, so that it is simple to become interested in the material and give it complete attention. A method such as SQ3R (Survey, Question, Read, Recite, Review) is a wonderful key to follow to make sure that the study habits are as effective as possible, especially in the case of learning from a textbook. Flashcards are great techniques for memorization. Learning to take good notes will mean that notes will be full of useful information, so that less sifting will need to be done to seek out what is pertinent for studying. Reviewing notes after class and then again on occasion will keep the information fresh in the mind. From notes that have been taken summary sheets and outlines can be made for simpler reviewing.

A study group can also be a very motivational and helpful place to study, as there will be a sharing of ideas, all of the minds can work together, to make sure that everyone understands, and the studying will be made more interesting because it will be a social occasion.

Basically, though, as long as the test-taker remains organized and self confident, with efficient study habits, less time will need to be spent studying, and higher grades will be achieved.

To become self confident, there are many useful steps. The first of these is "self talk." It has been shown through extensive research, that self-talk for students who suffer from test anxiety, should be well monitored, in order to make sure that it contributes to self confidence as opposed to sinking the student. Frequently the self talk of test-anxious students is negative or self-defeating, thinking that everyone else is smarter and faster, that they always mess up, and that if they don't do well, they'll fail the entire course. It is important to decreasing anxiety that awareness is made of self talk. Try writing any negative self thoughts and then disputing them with a positive statement instead. Begin self-encouragement as though it was a friend speaking. Repeat positive statements to help reprogram the mind to believing in successes instead of failures.

Helpful Techniques

Other extremely helpful techniques include:

Self-visualization of doing well and reaching goals
While aiming for an "A" level of understanding, don't try to "overprotect" by setting your expectations lower. This will only convince the mind to stop studying in order to meet the lower expectations.
Don't make comparisons with the results or habits of other students. These are individual factors, and different things work for different people, causing different results.
Strive to become an expert in learning what works well, and what can be done in order to improve. Consider collecting this data in a journal.
Create rewards for after studying instead of doing things before studying that will only turn into avoidance behaviors.
Make a practice of relaxing - by using methods such as progressive relaxation, self-hypnosis, guided imagery, etc - in order to make relaxation an automatic sensation.
Work on creating a state of relaxed concentration so that concentrating will take on the focus of the mind, so that none will be wasted on worrying.
Take good care of the physical self by eating well and getting enough sleep.
Plan in time for exercise and stick to this plan.

Beyond these techniques, there are other methods to be used before, during and after the test that will help the test-taker perform well in addition to overcoming anxiety.

Before the exam comes the academic preparation. This involves establishing a study schedule and beginning at least one week before the actual date of the test. By doing this, the anxiety of not having enough time to study for the test will be automatically eliminated. Moreover, this will make the studying a much more effective experience, ensuring that the learning will be an easier process. This relieves much undue pressure on the test-taker.

Summary sheets, note cards, and flash cards with the main concepts and examples of these main concepts should be prepared in advance of the actual studying time. A topic should never be eliminated from this process. By omitting a topic because it isn't expected to be on the test is only setting up the test-taker for anxiety should it actually appear on the exam. Utilize the course syllabus for laying out the topics that should be studied. Carefully go over the notes that were made in class, paying special attention to any of the issues that the professor took special care to emphasize while lecturing in class. In the textbooks, use the chapter review, or if possible, the chapter tests, to begin your review.

It may even be possible to ask the instructor what information will be covered on the exam, or what the format of the exam will be (for example, multiple choice, essay, free form, true-false). Additionally, see if it is possible to find out how many questions will be on the test. If a review sheet or sample test has been offered by the professor, make good use of it, above anything else, for the preparation for the test. Another great resource for getting to know the examination is reviewing tests from previous semesters. Use these tests to review, and aim to achieve a 100% score on each of the possible topics. With a few exceptions, the goal that you set for yourself is the highest one that you will reach.

Take all of the questions that were assigned as homework, and rework them to any other possible course material. The more problems reworked, the more skill and confidence will form as a result. When forming the solution to a problem, write out each of the steps. Don't simply do head work. By doing as many steps on paper as possible, much clarification and therefore confidence will be formed. Do this with as many homework problems as possible, before checking the answers. By checking the answer after each problem, a reinforcement will exist, that will not be on the exam. Study situations should be as exam-like as possible, to prime the test-taker's system for the experience. By waiting to check the answers at the end, a psychological advantage will be formed, to decrease the stress factor.

Another fantastic reason for not cramming is the avoidance of confusion in concepts, especially when it comes to mathematics. 8-10 hours of study will become one hundred percent more effective if it is spread out over a week or at least several days, instead of doing it all in one sitting. Recognize that the human brain requires time in order to assimilate new material, so frequent breaks and a span of study time over several days will be much more beneficial.

Additionally, don't study right up until the point of the exam. Studying should stop a minimum of one hour before the exam begins. This allows the brain to rest and put things in their proper order. This will also provide the time to become as relaxed as possible when going into the examination room. The test-taker will also have time to eat well and eat sensibly. Know that the brain needs food as much as the rest of the body. With enough food and enough sleep, as well as a relaxed attitude, the body and the mind are primed for success.

Avoid any anxious classmates who are talking about the exam. These students only spread anxiety, and are not worth sharing the anxious sentimentalities.

Before the test also involves creating a positive attitude, so mental preparation should also be a point of concentration. There are many keys to creating a positive attitude. Should fears become rushing in, make a visualization of taking the exam, doing well, and seeing an A written on the paper. Write out a list of affirmations that will bring a feeling of confidence, such as "I am doing well in my English class," "I studied well and know my material," "I enjoy this class." Even if the affirmations aren't believed at first, it sends a positive message to the subconscious which will result in an alteration of the overall belief system, which is the system that creates reality.

If a sensation of panic begins, work with the fear and imagine the very worst! Work through the entire scenario of not passing the test, failing the entire course, and dropping out of school, followed by not getting a job, and pushing a shopping cart through the dark alley where you'll live. This will place things into perspective! Then, practice deep breathing and create a visualization of the opposite situation - achieving an "A" on the exam, passing the entire course, receiving the degree at a graduation ceremony.

On the day of the test, there are many things to be done to ensure the best results, as well as the most calm outlook. The following stages are suggested in order to maximize test-taking potential:

Begin the examination day with a moderate breakfast, and avoid any coffee or beverages with caffeine if the test taker is prone to jitters. Even people who are used to managing caffeine can feel jittery or light-headed when it is taken on a test day.
Attempt to do something that is relaxing before the examination begins. As last minute cramming clouds the mastering of overall concepts, it is better to use this time to create a calming outlook.
Be certain to arrive at the test location well in advance, in order to provide time to select a location that is away from doors, windows and other distractions, as well as giving enough time to relax before the test begins.
Keep away from anxiety generating classmates who will upset the sensation of stability and relaxation that is being attempted before the exam.
Should the waiting period before the exam begins cause anxiety, create a self-distraction by reading a light magazine or something else that is relaxing and simple.

During the exam itself, read the entire exam from beginning to end, and find out how much time should be allotted to each individual problem. Once writing the exam, should more time be taken for a problem, it should be abandoned, in order to begin another problem. If there is time at the end, the unfinished problem can always be returned to and completed.

Read the instructions very carefully - twice - so that unpleasant surprises won't follow during or after the exam has ended.

When writing the exam, pretend that the situation is actually simply the completion of homework within a library, or at home. This will assist in forming a relaxed atmosphere, and will allow the brain extra focus for the complex thinking function.

Begin the exam with all of the questions with which the most confidence is felt. This will build the confidence level regarding the entire exam and will begin a quality momentum. This will also create encouragement for trying the problems where uncertainty resides.

Going with the "gut instinct" is always the way to go when solving a problem. Second guessing should be avoided at all costs. Have confidence in the ability to do well.

For essay questions, create an outline in advance that will keep the mind organized and make certain that all of the points are remembered. For multiple choice, read every answer, even if the correct one has been spotted - a better one may exist.

Continue at a pace that is reasonable and not rushed, in order to be able to work carefully. Provide enough time to go over the answers at the end, to check for small errors that can be corrected.

Should a feeling of panic begin, breathe deeply, and think of the feeling of the body releasing sand through its pores. Visualize a calm, peaceful place, and include all of the sights, sounds and sensations of this image. Continue the deep breathing, and take a few minutes to continue this with closed eyes. When all is well again, return to the test.

If a "blanking" occurs for a certain question, skip it and move on to the next question. There will be time to return to the other question later. Get everything done that can be done, first, to guarantee all the grades that can be compiled, and to build all of the confidence possible. Then return to the weaker questions to build the marks from there.

Remember, one's own reality can be created, so as long as the belief is there, success will follow. And remember: anxiety can happen later, right now, there's an exam to be written!

After the examination is complete, whether there is a feeling for a good grade or a bad grade, don't dwell on the exam, and be certain to follow through on the reward that was promised...and enjoy it! Don't dwell on any mistakes that have been made, as there is nothing that can be done at this point anyway.

Additionally, don't begin to study for the next test right away. Do something relaxing for a while, and let the mind relax and prepare itself to begin absorbing information again.

From the results of the exam - both the grade and the entire experience, be certain to learn from what has gone on. Perfect studying habits and work some more on confidence in order to make the next examination experience even better than the last one.

Learn to avoid places where openings occurred for laziness, procrastination and day dreaming.

Use the time between this exam and the next one to better learn to relax, even learning to relax on cue, so that any anxiety can be controlled during the next exam. Learn how to relax the body. Slouch in your chair if that helps. Tighten and then relax all of the different muscle groups, one group at a time, beginning with the feet and then working all the way up to the neck and face. This will ultimately relax the muscles more than they were to begin with. Learn how to breathe deeply and comfortably, and focus on this breathing going in and out as a relaxing thought. With every exhale, repeat the word "relax."

As common as test anxiety is, it is very possible to overcome it. Make yourself one of the test-takers who overcome this frustrating hindrance.

Special Report: Additional Bonus Material

Due to our efforts to try to keep this book to a manageable length, we've created a link that will give you access to all of your additional bonus material.

Please visit http://www.mometrix.com/bonus948/nhfoundread to access the information.